Build a Website for Free

Second Edition

Mark Bell

 800 East 96th Street,
Indianapolis, Indiana 46240

Build a Website for Free

ISBN-13: 978-0-7897-4718-1

ISBN-10: 0-7897-4718-9

The Library of Congress Cataloging-in-Publication data is on file.

2 3 4 5 6 7 8 DOC 15 14 13 12 11

Associate Publisher
Greg Wiegand

Acquisitions Editor
Laura Norman

Development Editor
Lora Baughey

Managing Editor
Kristy Hart

Senior Project Editor
Betsy Harris

Copy Editor
Karen A. Gill

Indexer
Erika Millen

Proofreader
Williams Woods Publishing Services

Technical Editor
Christian Kenyeres

Publishing Coordinator
Cindy Teeters

Book Designer
Anne Jones

Compositor
Nonie Ratcliff

Trademarks

All terms mentioned in this book that are known to be trademarks or service marks have been appropriately capitalized. Que Publishing cannot attest to the accuracy of this information. Use of a term in this book should not be regarded as affecting the validity of any trademark or service mark.

Warning and Disclaimer

Every effort has been made to make this book as complete and as accurate as possible, but no warranty or fitness is implied. The information provided is on an "as is" basis. The author and the publisher shall have neither liability nor responsibility to any person or entity with respect to any loss or damages arising from the information contained in this book.

Bulk Sales

Que Publishing offers excellent discounts on this book when ordered in quantity for bulk purchases or special sales. For more information, please contact

U.S. Corporate and Government Sales
1-800-382-3419
corpsales@pearsontechgroup.com

For sales outside the United States, please contact

International Sales
international@pearson.com

Contents at a Glance

Table of Contents

About the Author

Mark Bell is a Ph.D. student at Indiana University. He studies media and its effect on social relations. Before returning to school, Mark worked for 15 years in the software industry as a technical writer, trainer, and developer. He started his first web design company in 1993 and has been making pages and managing websites ever since. He is the father of Jackson, 8, and the husband of Sarah "Intellagirl" Robbins. Mark blogs at blog.markwbell.com. You can find him on Twitter, Facebook, and LinkedIn.

Dedication

To three people:

To Sarah, my wife, who because she believes in my strength and determination fuels those two things. She gives me energy, life, and love. I am damn lucky to have found her.

To my son Jackson, who is a constant source of joy and inspiration. He surprises me every day with his warmth and intelligence. Son, I give my best to you.

To my friend Davin, who has always stood by me and loved me no matter what. He is a true friend who has joined me in this digital journey from the beginning with a Timex Sinclair 1000 in his living room.

Acknowledgments

This book was written by one person but had the contributions of thousands from the web via Twitter.com and Facebook. It also comes with the help of Sarah, my wife, and mental collaborators Travis, Jim, and Nick. Without these great minds around me, I would never get anywhere.

Special thanks to Matt who worked with me on this book, finding holes and rough patches and taking screen shots. It's been an honor to work with you.

Special thanks to Indiana University and my advisor, Harmeet Sawhney, for understanding that I need to make money doing "other" projects. To John Dailey, for letting me learn how to teach the web from a master.

Thanks to Tim Berners-Lee for creating the web and for Richard Stallman for being the father of open source, and to all the open-source developers who put in millions of hours so that we all can share amazing free software.

Thanks to my high school computer teachers, Mrs. Todd and Mr. Cooper, who let me run wild in a digital playground.

To my mother, brothers, sisters, and all their families.

Most special thanks to my friends and family, who are patient with my writing schedule.

We Want to Hear from You!

As the reader of this book, you are our most important critic and commentator. We value your opinion and want to know what we're doing right, what we could do better, what areas you'd like to see us publish in, and any other words of wisdom you're willing to pass our way.

As an associate publisher for Que Publishing, I welcome your comments. You can email or write me directly to let me know what you did or didn't like about this book—as well as what we can do to make our books better.

Please note that I cannot help you with technical problems related to the topic of this book. We do have a User Services group, however, where I will forward specific technical questions related to the book.

When you write, please be sure to include this book's title and author as well as your name, email address, and phone number. I will carefully review your comments and share them with the author and editors who worked on the book.

Email: feedback@quepublishing.com

Mail: Greg Wiegand
         Associate Publisher
         Que Publishing
         800 East 96th Street
         Indianapolis, IN 46240 USA

Reader Services

Visit our website and register this book at quepublishing.com/register for convenient access to any updates, downloads, or errata that might be available for this book.

Introduction

So you want to build a website for free?

If you are reading this book, you probably want to build a website (even though you might not know exactly what that is), and you want to do it for free. If you have no idea what a website really is and need some basic information, you'll learn this later in the Introduction. If you know what a website is, you probably are more interested in the "free" part. All the software and tools I discuss in this book are free of charge. If at all possible, I choose the best free alternative to commercial software.

In the past decade, the Internet, and in particular the World Wide Web, has grown considerably. There are now millions of websites on the Internet covering all sorts of subjects, from family and business to education and entertainment. Some websites have been long-lasting and useful (Yahoo.com and Google.com), and others disappear as quickly as they come. You might have plans to create a website that you hope millions of people will go to, or your site's purpose might be just to stay connected to your family members.

Why This Book?

You probably picked up this book because you have an idea in your head—an idea you want to share on the World Wide Web in the form of a website. You might have a fully formed idea or just a kernel of that idea, but you have a starting point. Maybe you have been given the job of creating a website and have no idea where to start, or maybe you have a burning desire to connect with other people.

Regardless of your reason for creating a site, this book will help you understand the process of how those ideas become a website and then walk you through creating five different sites for specific purposes. These sites include a basic website, a blog, a content management system, a wiki, and a multimedia website. You might not know or care about all these, but this book will show you how to build them for free. This book covers how to plan, design, build, and maintain a website, and it does it using free tools. With simple step-by-step instructions, you will be up and running on the World Wide Web before you know it.

For Free, Really?

You're probably wondering how much this is going to cost. The book title says "free," but you have never believed anything was really free. This book is unique.

Different people and websites will promise you the lowest prices possible on website tools, hosting, and creation. Conventional wisdom says nothing is free. Generally, the more you invest in a project, the more options you have.

In the past five years, though, open-source and free software have been flooding the World Wide Web and allowing people to create fun, interesting, dynamic web pages for very little money. This book tries to use free software as much as possible. If people are giving away quality software, you should use it.

Open-Source Software

In the previous section, I threw out the term "open-source software," and you're probably wondering what the heck that is.

Most software, including your operating system, word processor, and web browser, is more than likely developed according to a traditional software model. Software is traditionally created by a bunch of guys who run a software company, which runs on money. The people who run the company pay programmers to write and test software, and they employ marketing and salespeople to sell their products to you, the consumer. Most software has been developed this way since the mid-1980s.

The Internet is in a constant state of flux. Some people call this a revolution and others just a fad, but in reality, open source is here to stay. Open-source software is created by teams of people working for free, and it is given away to anyone for free. More than that, open-source projects also give away the parts that make up software, or "source code," which a traditional company keeps secret. The theory behind all this is that the more people programming, editing, and using the open-source software, the better it becomes. Also, when the work is distributed among thousands of people, most of whom will never meet, the workload per person is drastically reduced. Don't tell the traditional software industry, but their programmers are working for them and then going home at night and doing the same thing for free!

In this book, as much as possible, we will be using open-source software because it is usually free and, surprisingly, is some of the highest-quality stuff available. There are open-source operating systems, web browsers, graphics applications, and even website management tools. All these are covered in this book.

With each piece of software I recommend, I list where to find the latest version and what the major features are.

Is This Legal?

Your next question might be, "If I am getting this stuff for free, isn't that stealing?" I am not advocating or recommending that anyone steal or pirate software. All the software I recommend is given away for free. The software industry is full of hard-working people who deserve to be paid for their work. If there is a price for software, I tell you about it. Where there is a cost, I provide a free alternative and let you know the differences.

I Can't Really Do This...Can I?

In my years of teaching software in the corporate and academic world, I have heard people say they can't do some computer task that they need or want to do because of this or that reason. Some people say they are afraid of computers or "just don't get them," some blame the hardware, and some just say they can't understand these crazy things. This book is designed to get even the most apprehensive would-be website developer, who has no special qualifications or knowledge, up and running in no time. I explain each task to you in easy-to-understand instructions.

Note on Edition 2

Any book about the web or the Internet in general is out of date as soon as it is finished. The World Wide Web continues to change at an accelerated rate. This book is no exception. For this reason, a new edition has been created to update the text. As part of my revisions, all the links have been checked and new ones added. Also, the mobile web has exploded in use and market share. The tablet market looks like a possible contender for the next big thing, so I have added sections on the iPad also.

How to Use This Book

Throughout this book, you will find special little notes to help you along the way.

Tips and Cautions

tip **Tips** contain little bits of information that will give you extra knowledge or save you time or money. They don't present mandatory information, but you should pay attention to them.

caution **Cautions**, on the other hand, are important to pay attention to. A Caution is must-read information that you need to know before proceeding with the task at hand. Please pay close attention to them.

Geek Speak

The world of computers and the culture that surrounds them are full of jargon. It is almost as though acronyms and arcane terms are the fuel that the software industry uses. When the terminology gets techy in the book, the Geek Speak sections decipher the lingo for you and use common, simple words to explain what is going on.

> ## 🎤 Geek Speak
> These notes act as a mini-translator into the world of computer geeks.

Whenever a line of code is too long to fit on one printed line, we've broken it and used a code-continuation arrow to indicate the continuation:

```
<param name="movie" value="http://www.youtube.com/v/
➥-xL7YSsEyOs?fs=1&amp;hl=en_US"></param>
```

Web 101

This book is trying to make it as simple and cheap as possible for you to create a website. To make sure this can happen, it's important to cover some basics, including how the Internet and web work. You may use the Internet every day but not know what it really is. For me, a basic understanding of the building blocks of the web helps me build better websites.

If you already know how the Internet works and what a web page and website are, skip ahead to Chapter 1, "The Order of Things." But if you want a quick refresher on some basic Internet facts, read over this section before moving on to the rest of the book.

What Is the Internet?

Can you even remember a time before the Internet existed? Depending on your age, the answer may vary, but how did we ever get along without it? Think about trying to find a new restaurant to go to before the Internet was around. You would have to look in the Restaurant section of the Yellow Pages, use a map to find the street where the restaurant was, and then devise your own directions to get there. With the Internet, you can not only do most of that with the click of a button, but you can read the menu, see pictures of the interior, and maybe even make reservations—all without leaving the house or picking up the phone. But what *is* this incredibly useful thing we call the Internet?

The Internet is simply the largest network of computers in existence. All these computers speak a similar language and share information easily. That's it. You don't need to know the history or the technology beyond that. When your modem connects you to the Internet, your computer becomes part of the computer network known as the Internet. You might have a local network at work or home, but that local network is connected to the Internet.

What Is the World Wide Web?

People talk about the web and the Internet as if they were the same thing. They aren't. As mentioned previously, the Internet is a network of computers. The World Wide Web is a method of viewing the information on those networked computers. The World Wide Web is a collection of certain files on certain computers in the network of computers. These files contain information that, when referred to collectively, is called the *World Wide Web* (see Figure I.1).

Geek Speak

www

Ever wonder why so many pages start with "www"? Those letters are just technical shorthand to tell your web browser you are looking for something on the World Wide Web. The www isn't even needed, though. Most web browsers will find the site whether you type www or not.

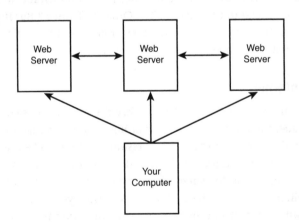

FIGURE I.1

The Internet is made of web servers to which you connect with your computer.

What Is a Web Page?

The World Wide Web is then made up of web pages. A web page is a file of information that can be accessed and displayed on your computer. When you access the file, it is downloaded to your computer. When you go to Amazon.com, you are accessing a file on an Amazon computer, it is downloaded, and the information in that file is displayed on your computer. When you go surfing on the web, you are connecting to a bunch of different computers, all transferring files to your computer.

What Is a Website?

Basically, a website is a collection of web pages (see Figure I.2) stored on a particular computer (called a web server) and accessed by outside computers. The site creator puts the files on the web server. A web server is just a computer with special software that allows others to view your web page when they go to the address of the web server. When you go to cnn.com, there is a collection of pages that make up the website for the CNN television network.

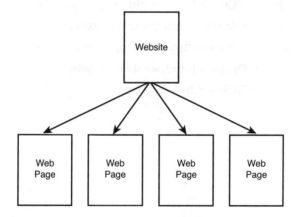

FIGURE I.2

A website is made of web pages.

What Is a Web Browser?

A web browser is a piece of software on your computer or mobile device that you use to access web pages on websites. All desktop computers include at least one web browser as part of the preinstalled software. A web browser is the tool you use to view websites, and more and more often it is also a tool to help you create websites.

All browsers work essentially the same way. You enter a website address into the browser or click on a link. This tells the browser to go to that Internet address and download the files (images, text, videos) to your computer or mobile device. Then these files are displayed in a way that looks good (hopefully) and allows you to interact with them.

Several browsers are available to you. A good website developer (that's you) will be familiar with all the major types, and more than likely will have them installed on a computer used for testing. More than ever, people are using mobile browser to view the web. Your phone probably has a web browser in it. Keep in mind, Safari on a Mac is not the same as Safari on the iPhone. If you are serious about web development, you need to get and keep the latest versions of browser software on your computer. You also need to be aware of each browser's unique features and limitations. The most common browsers are as follows:

- **Internet Explorer (Microsoft)**—http://www.microsoft.com/ie/
- **Chrome (Google)**—http://chrome.google.com
- **Firefox (Mozilla)**—http://www.firefox.com
- **Safari (Apple)**—http://www.apple.com/safari/
- **Opera (Opera)**—http://www.opera.com/
- **Flock (Flock)**—http://flock.com/

The Basics

The Order of Things

I t is important before beginning to build a website to have some idea of the completed project. Think of it this way: If you are going on vacation, you have a chosen destination, a method of travel, a route, and a time table. Without any one of these things, your vacation will probably be less than enjoyable. Each of the parts is also interconnected. If you are planning on flying but don't have a destination, you won't be able to define a time table. Building a website is a similar process. It's a common temptation to want to build your site as soon as possible, but as is the case with traveling, if you get on the road with no sense of your destination, you are going to get lost quickly. Also, the parts of the project have an order to them. You can't go to an amusement park at your destination until you have mapped out its location. Similarly, knowing and following the order of these interconnected steps allows your plan to be a success.

In this chapter, we look at the steps for the entire website creation process, from planning to maintenance, in a brief but fundamental way. Don't be tempted to skip to the next chapter just because this is an overview. These steps are the foundational building blocks in the process of creating your best website.

IN THIS CHAPTER

■ The Website Creation Process

1

Each part of the process is covered in greater detail later on, but it helps to have an overview of the whole process before you begin.

The Website Creation Process

In this book, the creation and maintenance of a website is broken down into a process, which you should follow as closely as possible. This process is the result of knowledge gained from building my own websites and hours of discussion with successful web designers. Following these steps will help you immensely as the process continues. All the steps in website creation and maintenance require work and thought, but they don't necessarily involve a computer or any technology. These steps are outlined in Figure 1.1 and then detailed in chapters later in the book.

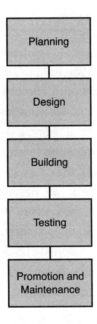

FIGURE 1.1

The website creation process.

1. Planning

All endeavors should start with a planning phase. You have to plan the steps needed to complete a project. The way I think of it, a project such as creating a website is made up of small steps that, when done correctly, result in a successful project.

1

This might be the easiest thing to skip, but it certainly is as important, and might actually be more important, than any other part of the process. By making plans and decisions early on, you will find that the later steps in the process are easier and seem more guided.

The following are some things you need to decide before you begin:

- Why am I building this website?
- How do I want this website to function?
- What goals do I have for the website?
- Is this a website I expect people to come to once or return to often?
- Who is going to design, build, test, and maintain the website?
- What tools will be used to build the website?
- What is my website budget?
- Who do I want to visit my website?

→ For more on planning and the things you need to plan for, **see** Chapter 3, "Planning Your Site."

2. Design

There are as many ways to design a website as there are ideas for content and designers building those sites. When I talk about web design, I mean more than just the look of the website. Design is more than just graphics. It also includes the way the pages are organized (site structure), the buttons or links that enable the site visitor to get to those pages (navigation elements), and technical details such as how the programming language is used and which application technologies will be employed. When I design a website, I use a whiteboard to draw out what my page will look like.

Everyone wants a unique website, so it is important for you to look at as many websites as you can before planning and designing your own. This will give you insight into trends that look fresh and new and which tired web clichés to avoid.

The key to creating an excellent website is taking your unique content and matching it to an excellent design. Chapter 4, "Designing Your Site," covers many design decisions you have to make, as well as some trends in websites that have enduring qualities.

→ For more on web design, **see** Chapter 4.

3. Building

Far too often people start at this phase without doing the planning and design needed to create a successful website. Building is the actual work of creating pages, editing graphics, making links, managing multimedia, and adding scripts and other elements to the server.

In the past, a website needed to be created by hand. This meant that a developer had to manually type each file that made up the website. Luckily for you, this is no longer the case. The building section covers web page creation tools, graphics tools, and other utilities that enable you to quickly create a single page or an entire site without writing a single line of code. Most of these utilities and tools are free or very cheap.

If you have done your planning and design, turn to Chapter 7, "Elements of a Website," to begin building your site. Once you start building your website, see Chapter 6, "Moving Files to and from the Internet," to move the files onto your web server.

→   For more on building your website, **see** Part III, "Website Building Basics."

4. Testing

Testing? No one told you there would be a test. What I mean by testing is ensuring that everything on your website works. Some of the things you should test include navigation (moving from page to page in the site), graphics, and content (be sure no information is missing from your pages). You also need to get into the habit of testing and retesting your website with each change you make, even after your site is up and running. There are free tools available that help you do this.

→   For more on testing your website, **see** Chapter 16, "Testing Your Website."

5. Promotion and Maintenance

After you have planned, designed, built, and tested your website, you are ready to send it out into the world. This is not the end of the story, though. You need to promote your website to others, make sure it appears on *search engines*, and promote it to people you don't know. However, doing

Geek Speak

search engine

A search engine is a website that allows you to search for other websites.

all of that is still not enough. You need to maintain and update your site so that people have a reason to come back to it.

For details on how to promote and continue work on your website, see Chapters 17 and 18.

Choosing a Location for Your Site

Web Hosting

One of the most common questions people have when they set out to create a website is where to host it.

Remember that a website is a collection of web pages, graphics, script files, and anything else associated with the website. These files need to be stored on a computer that is accessible to other people. This computer that other people can access is also called a server or a host. When a server stores your files and allows others to access them, it can be said to be hosting your website. Deciding where to host your website's files is extremely important and should be planned and researched like any other part of the process.

note This section is chock-ful of geek speak. I have explained the technical terms throughout this chapter so you understand the technology and therefore make the right web hosting choice.

What Is a Web Server?

A web server is a computer that stores and shares web files. Other people access these web files with their web browser.

You access servers every time you go to any web page. You type in the address of the server, it sends you the version of the web files it has stored on its hard drive, and voilá—you see the web page. A web server has three basic functions:

- **Storage**—A web server stores web files on a hard drive. Every web page, graphic, and script needs to be stored on a web server.
- **Share Files**—Based on the requests that a web server gets, it provides the files over the Internet to a viewer's browser.
- **Analytics**—A good web server keeps track of all the people accessing the website's files and captures data about them. This can be incredibly useful and is talked about more in Chapter 18, "Maintaining Your Website."

When you put your website's files onto a server, the company that owns the servers is "hosting" your site.

A number of different server options may be available to you (see Figure 2.1). The rest of this section covers what to look for when making decisions about hosting your website. It is important to do this during the planning stage because the features or limitations of your hosting choice may influence your site when it comes time to build it.

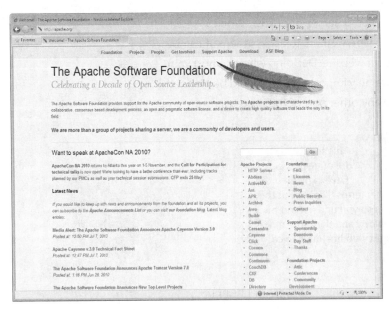

FIGURE 2.1

Apache is an example of a free web server. You can find information about it at www.apache.org.

Determining Your Web Hosting Needs

Before you decide on the hosting option that is right for you, it's good to assess your needs for that hosting company. The following sections discuss some things you might want to consider.

Cost

Hosting your website files and making them accessible to other people can cost money. As with many of these considerations, a wide range of pricing is available, from close to free to more than a mortgage payment a month. Don't think that any web hosting is completely free, though. Even if you host your own web server out of your home, you still need to buy the equipment and pay your electric bill, rent, and yourself.

Try to decide on a budget you can spend on an ongoing basis to have your website hosted. For my money, a little bit of monthly fee solves so many problems and offers so many opportunities it is well worth it.

Technical Knowledge Required

Different hosting options provide different features and require you to have a higher level of technical skills than others. Honestly assess your technical skills and the time you're willing to spend using these skills before choosing a hosting option.

Maintenance Needs

It's important to know who is maintaining your web server. If you are doing it, you need to perform several regular maintenance tasks yourself. This includes making sure the server is running, that it is accessible to other people, and that it has the latest software installed. If you are using a hosting service, someone else might do this for you, but probably for a fee. You need to evaluate how much time you can give to maintaining a web server or how much you are willing to spend.

Storage Space

Your web files take up digital space. You need to know the amount of space you have available to store and back-up your files. Unless you are the only website on the web server, you need to find out how much space you have available on that server, when and if it is backed-up.

Accessibility

How easy is it to upload and access your files on the web server? Do you have remote access to the server? In other words, can you connect to it from any other computer, or do you need to have physical access to it? This can make a huge difference if your access is limited or restricted in any way. Also, you should know what security requirements (such as personal information) you have to give the web hosting service for security reasons.

Bandwidth Needs

Bandwidth determines how much information can be transmitted over a period of time. Every time your website is downloaded it uses up some of the bandwidth the web server allots to you. One way to think of it is how many times your website files can be downloaded. Some web hosting services put a limit on the amount of bandwidth your website requires.

With some hosting options, bandwidth is nearly unlimited, and with others it is restricted. If you expect a lot of people to come to your website, pay careful attention to the web hosting bandwidth restrictions.

Domain Name Service

A *domain name* is an address on the Internet. It references a particular server where a website is stored. See the Geek Speak sidebar for further explanation of domain names.

You need to know whether your hosting option will take care of domain name services and, if so, at what cost. Domain name services include registering and hosting your domain name so that other computers on the Internet know to come to your web host when they type in your URL.

Domain names are also used for email addresses. Check to see if the ISP provides email addresses for domains also.

 **Geek Speak**

domain name

A domain name is just a fancy way of referring to the words that act as a website's address. There are a number of computers on the Internet that keep all the domain names straight. These computers take the domain name you enter in your browser and find the right web server. A hosting service usually collects the information needed to register your domain name.

Hosting Options

After you have some idea of what you are looking for in a hosting option, you should look around and research what is available. There are several options, so carefully match your web hosting needs with the right hosting option. The following sections describe some hosting options.

Home Hosting

It's possible to host your own web server at home. At the very least you would need a dedicated web server machine, a dedicated always-on high-speed Internet connection, server software, and the technical know-how and time to install, configure, and maintain your own server, not to mention secure it. Tired yet? This option is usually for hard-core geeks, but yes, it is possible to host your web server from your own home.

> **tip** For an excellent explanation of setting up a home web host, look at http://lifehacker.com/software/feature/how-to-set-up-a-personal-home-web-server-124212.php
>
> www.diywebserver.com/

Free Online Hosting

Some website hosting sites, such as Google Sites, allow free hosting for websites. They can offer this because they limit the storage, pages, and files you can put on their sites. Google Sites, for example, takes care of all the hosting for free but does not allow you any domain name service and allows a very limited amount of content. If you don't want any web hosting hassles and have low technology needs, this might be the option for you.

Online Hosting Service

Several companies offer web hosting for a reasonable cost ($10 to $20 U.S. a month, plus setup fees). These services look after the servers and allow you a wide range of website possibilities. They usually have a number of different hosting plans, based on what you need in terms of domain and other technical services (things like physically maintaining the web server and installing new software versions).

This is the kind of hosting I use for my websites.

Professional Hosting

If you are expecting a huge amount of hosting and high technical customization needs, you might want to consider professional hosting. For a large sum of money, a hosting company rents you your own server and maintains it for you. This gives you a huge range of possibilities, but it is expensive.

Commercial Hosting

If you are creating a website for your company, there might be people within your company who can host and maintain your web server. If your boss asks you to create a website, try to find out whether a system is already in place for site hosting.

So What Works Best for You?

To help you pick the hosting option that fits your needs, I have summarized the possible needs described in this chapter in an easy-to-use reference shown in Table 2.1. You probably won't find a perfect solution (the perfect solution being all features and services for free), but you can match the needs and options as closely as possible.

Table 2.1   Web Hosting Options

	Cost	Technical Knowledge Needed	Maintenance	Storage Space	Accessibility	Bandwidth Needs	Domain Name Service
Home Hosting	Low–Medium	High	High	Low–High	High	Low	Medium
Free Online	Low	Low	Low	Low	Low	High	Low
Online Hosting Service	Low–Medium	Low–Medium	Low	Medium–High	Medium	High	High
Professional Hosting	High	Low–Medium	Low	High	Medium	High	High
Commercial Hosting	Low–High	Low–High	Low–Medium	Medium–High	High	Medium–High	Medium–High

Working with Different Types of Hosting Services

After you have chosen the type of hosting you want, your job might not be complete. In fact, you might spend as much time researching the available services as you did choosing the type of hosting.

Free Services

Several free hosting services exist on the Internet. I profile a couple of them here, but this is by no means a complete list, and new site hosts show up every day. Before signing up, review the features of the site and the terms of service and use, read reviews of the service, and if possible, look at sites that use the free hosting service. Remember that although all these sites will host your website for free, they do come with limitations. The following sections describe a few of the best free services for web hosting.

Like in school, I have given the websites a letter grade for ease of use and features. A grade of A is excellent. A grade of B is good. A grade of C is satisfactory, and a grade of D is unsatisfactory.

Google Sites (sites.google.com)

Ease of Use: A

Features: B

Google Sites makes things as free and easy as its search engine is. Google's emphasis with Google Sites is connecting people in groups as easily as possible. If you are interested in Google Sites make sure to watch the introduction tutorial.

Google Sites (see Figure 2.2) allows easy text editing, attachments, and comments. The page creation tool allows easy linking, addition of images, and creation of new pages. It has page templates for commonly created pages with programming already added. Google also allows you to let other people change your site if you are working on the website as a team.

You can easily customize your pages and no HTML is required. If you like Google Sites, it also offers expanded services for a monthly fee.

→   For more on Google Sites, **see** Chapter 9, "Web Page Services."

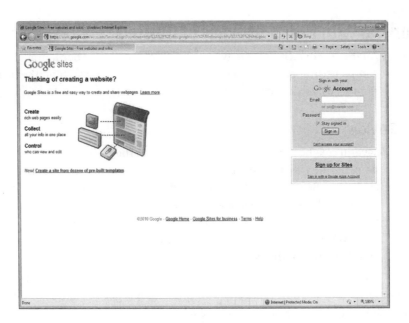

FIGURE 2.2

Google Sites makes the creation of websites fast, easy, and cheap.

Bravenet Hosting (www.bravenet.com/webhosting/hosting.php)

Ease of Use: B

Features: D

Bravenet offers a limited free hosting service. This is more of an introduction to its pay services but if you are in desperate need of free hosting it may work, in a pinch. Setup is fairly easy, but it allows next-to-no features for your website and a limited amount of space and bandwidth.

To allow for free service, Bravenet places ads on your page. If you are not interested in allowing ads on your site, Bravenet offers ad-free site hosting, for a fee, which also includes more features.

Windows Live Spaces (home.spaces.live.com)

Ease of Use: A

Features: D

Microsoft's Windows Live Spaces (see Figure 2.3) offers a space for MSN or Microsoft Live users to store photos, lists, and blog entries. It is limited in its features but is simple to use. In essence, it is not really hosting any kind of website, but it does give you a web presence if you want a simple one.

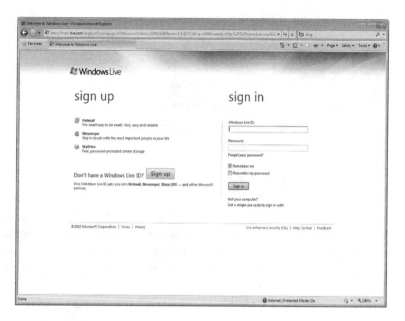

FIGURE 2.3

Microsoft's free pages include applications it calls gadgets.

JustFree (www.justfree.com/)

Ease of Use: B

Features: A

JustFree offers you a place to host your website files. It also offers more technical features, such as running PHP scripts and connecting to a MySQL database. If you don't know what those things are, don't worry—you don't need to. The idea here is that you need some technical knowledge to use the advanced features of this site.

JustFree limits the number of files and amount of bandwidth you can use, but those limits are more than adequate for a simple website. If you have some technical skills but no money, this may be the option for you.

Low-Cost Commercial Sites

If you are doing anything more than the basics, you probably should spend some money on a low-cost commercial web hosting company. If you are going to spend any money on your website, I would make this the first place you go. A good hosting company can give you so much in terms of features, space, and peace of mind that it makes the low monthly fee well worth it.

Here are a few of the better-known low-cost commercial sites. They all have tons of features and make setting up an excellent website much easier.

- DreamHost (www.dreamhost.com)
- Go Daddy (www.godaddy.com)
- Host Gator (www.hostgator.com/)
- A Small Orange (www.asmallorange.com)
- Blue Host (www.bluehost.com)

Other Resources

One thing I keep coming back to in this book is that people are using the web to give out and collect information like never before. When trying to decide which web hosting service to go with, take the time to read what people are saying about it. Substantiate the claims each service makes by researching the service.

You might find that a web service that sounds too good to be true actually adds viruses or other harmful software to your computer or website. In addition, new web hosting services appear constantly on the Internet. Keeping track of them all would be impossible, so let someone else do it for you. Web hosting sites are always being reviewed, and here are some of the websites that review those services:

- **Free Web Hosting (www.free-webhosts.com)**—A rating site for free web hosting services
- **FreeWebspace.net (www.freewebspace.net)**—A searchable guide to free web hosting
- **FindMyHost (http://findmyhost.com)**—Reviews and ratings of web hosting services
- **Webhosting Geeks (http://webhostinggeeks.com)**—Web hosting reviews from a more technical perspective

PART

Plan and Prep

Planning Your Site

The central question you need to answer before beginning any website project is "Why do you want to build a website?" Sometimes the answer can be simple—the boss wants you to create a site, you want to connect to old school friends, or you want to promote your home-based business. By asking the question, you can begin to figure out the best structure for the site you are building. For example, if you are making a website for your home based-business, you want your products and services on pages by themselves. You should also make sure the business contact information is on every page.

What follows in this section are some questions you should ask when planning your website's structure. You should try to answer as many of them as you can because they will help you make important decisions about your site. Don't just read the questions and think about the answers; make notes and develop a formal plan. If you are building this site for someone else, that person probably wants to see your plan of action. This plan of action would include listing the website's goals, the rough plans for the site and the pages, and a timeline of when you plan to complete the work.

What Type of Site Do You Want to Build?

As we all know, there are so many websites on the Internet that it is impossible to keep track of all of them. We use websites to book plane reservations, talk to friends, and catch up on the scores of last night's games. When you're thinking about why you are creating a website, you also need to figure out what kind of site it will be. The best way to familiarize yourself with types of websites is to look around on the web. Typically you go to the web with a particular objective in mind, such as renting a car or sending an email. This purpose sometimes causes you to overlook the structure and purpose of the sites you are viewing. Take another look at some of your favorite websites, and pay close attention to the structure and purpose of these sites. You'll be surprised by what you learn.

Types of Sites

New types of websites show up every day and are limited only by the imagination of the people creating them. Listed here are a few high-level types. If your website fits into one of these categories, read the listing and go to the example sites, paying close attention to the structure and design of each website.

- **Business**—In the early days of the web, there was a virtual gold rush of companies and corporations to the web thinking they could make a fortune overnight. This, of course, happened to only a few, but slowly over the past decade, businesses have begun to figure out how to make money, attract new customers, and find working business models. In fact, these days it is almost impossible to think of a business that doesn't have a website, from huge corporations to the mom-and-pop web shop down the street.

  Examples:

  - Amazon.com
  - Kodak.com (see Figure 3.1)
  - Bloomingfoods: www.bloomingfoods.coop/

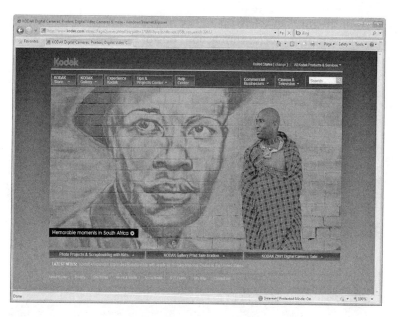

FIGURE 3.1

Kodak.com is an excellent business site.

- **Personal**—Before business invaded the World Wide Web, people were creating personal websites. These included family websites, fan sites, and journal sites such as blogs. This is really part of the World Wide Web's greatest cultural effects. Everyone can now have a voice on the web. You don't have to have a million dollars to have a great website that attracts lots of attention. From the rich and famous to the mom down the street, folks are making personal websites.

  Examples:
  - www.stephenfry.com
  - blog.markwbell.com
  - wonkette.com

- **Social**—Ever since computers have become connected to one another, they have become tools for social interactions. They make it simple for people to talk to each other online through social networking sites and email sites. The web is becoming more social every day. No longer is the Internet solely the refuge of geeks, but now just about everyone is making social connections one of the most dominant forces on the web.

Examples:

- Facebook.com (see Figure 3.2)
- Gmail.com
- Blogger.com

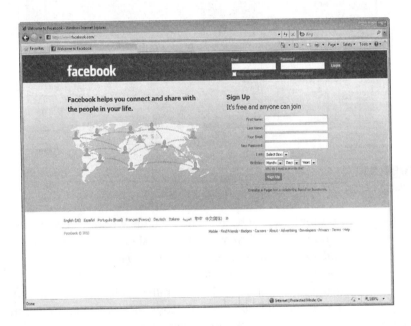

FIGURE 3.2

Have you been to Facebook today?

- **Informational**—The Internet is a storehouse of information. Some sites exist purely to give you free information. This information is so incredibly helpful that it is changing knowledge and education on a daily basis. The web has terabytes of information added it to every day—so much that you can never keep up on it all.

Examples:

- www.wikipedia.org (see Figure 3.3)
- www.imdb.com

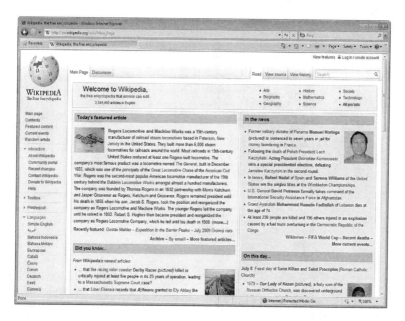

FIGURE 3.3

Wikipedia is the largest open-sourced reference work ever created.

Learning from Sites You Go To

As I mentioned earlier, you might need to try a new perspective to see the web for its structure rather than just its content. The following exercise forces you into that perspective and lets you see websites you visit in new ways:

1. Open your browser and look in your web history, which is a list of websites you have been to recently. It is usually found in a menu item. In Internet Explorer or Firefox, use Ctrl+Shift+H (see Figure 3.4).

2. Open the past few sites you have visited.

3. As you go through each site, ask yourself

   ■ What type of website is this?

   ■ What makes up the parts of the website?

   ■ How do you move between pages?

   ■ What gives you a sense that this website is one complete site and distinct from other sites on the Internet?

FIGURE 3.4

Explorer with History open.

You might even take notes on these websites. What makes these sites work? Or better yet, if you find a bad website, figure out what makes it bad, and don't make the same mistakes. Can you map out the structure of the website on a piece of paper?

Website Goals

Before you begin designing or building your website, you need an idea of what you want to achieve with it. The goals you are hoping to achieve will help you make decisions down the road.

Your goals are simply the things you want to accomplish with your website. These could be things such as making money, attracting attention, or making a statement. You should have goals for your site itself and for its content (see Figure 3.5). You also should think of short- and long-term goals for your site. Start by examining some of your favorite sites and determining the goals of those websites.

Ask yourself

- What is the overall goal of this website?
- What parts of the website show me this goal?
- Will my website be similar to or different from this site?

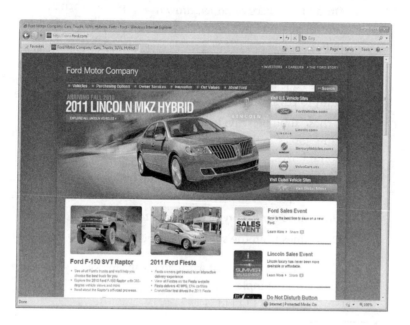

FIGURE 3.5

The goals of the Ford Motor Company website are to provide information about its products and to sell vehicles.

Organizing Websites

When you are figuring out the structure of your site, you need to think about both the site as a whole and each page. Remember that a website is just a collection of web pages. There should be a unity to what you create. This unity should be apparent on the site itself and on each page. For example, if you create a family website with pages for each member of the family (mom, dad, son, and daughter), each of those pages should look similar to the others. They should look like a united whole. If every page is different, the site visitor might get lost. You might start by looking at your entire site, or you could look at just one page.

Organizing the Site

When I begin to plan out a new website, I start with a blank piece of paper on which I draw out the website in this manner:

1. On a blank piece of paper, draw a central box and put Home Page in it.

2. Draw separate boxes around the Home Page box for subtopics you want to cover on the website.

3. If these subtopics divide further, add those topics to the page using additional boxes.

4. Determine what warrants a separate page. A web page should have its own unique content that is equal in amount to that of other pages.

5. Draw lines connecting these pages to the Home Page box.

6. Draw lines from the subtopics of each page to the page itself.

Now you have a rough map of what you want to do on your website. See Figure 3.6 for an example.

Geek Speak

home page

A *home page* is the first page people see when they come to your website. This page is the one loaded when people type in your domain address. Keep in mind that people do not stay long at any website—usually just seconds—so this is where they get their first impression.

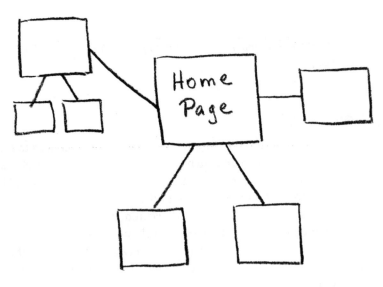

FIGURE 3.6

A rough map of a website.

Organizing the Page

In the same way as the site, I begin organizing each web page with a hand-drawn template. I keep it as simple and generic as possible so I can then make each page look like a unified page in a website. This is the method I use:

1. On another blank piece of paper, draw a rectangle that is longer than wide and fills most of the page. This rectangle represents a web page that is viewed with a typical browser on a typical screen.

2. At the top of this page, draw a horizontal line across the page, about 15% of the way down. This is your *header*.

3. At the bottom of this page, draw another horizontal line across the page, about 15% of the way up. This is your *footer*.

4. Add a rough outline of how you want your content to look on your site. You might want to have columns or tables. Take some time to express your creativity. Figure 3.7 gives you a general idea of how your site should look.

Geek Speak

header and footer

The header and footer sections of the page are the same for every page. Typically you'll find links to other pages and contact information in the header and footer. Look at other web pages, and you will see many have headers and footers.

You may have the same organizational structure for your whole website, or you might have a couple of different ones for different parts. This is essentially a paper template. A template allows you to keep consistency across multiple pages. Let your content define the structure.

FIGURE 3.7
Web page diagram.

Best Practices of Website Organization

There are some general rules, or best practices, for organizing a website that you should keep in mind as you organize your site. These rules are not the law but will help you avoid common mistakes.

Keep Your Website Simple

Above all, especially when beginning the planning for your website, keep things as simple as possible. Try not to make your website too complicated right away. You can always add things later. A simple website allows your message to be clearly understood and your goals easily attained (see Figure 3.8). If you get too complex too quickly, your visitors will get lost.

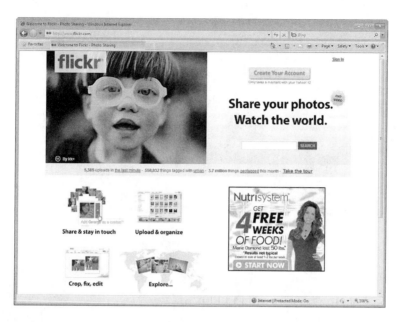

FIGURE 3.8
flickr is a clean and well-organized website.

Keep Your Website Consistent

Try to keep your website a unified whole. This makes it look more professional and helps the transmission of your message. A website filled with inconsistent pages makes for a mess that drives visitors away. A site that is unified and consistent from page to page conveys the fact that the creator of the website has invested a great deal of time to present a well-crafted and well-conceived site whose purpose is for your enjoyment. Keep your pages uncluttered and organized. Use consistent structures on pages (such as headers and footers) so your visitors can easily tell what your website is about and not get lost in a bunch of unorganized text and links.

Keep Your Website Easy to Maintain

Well-organized, well-designed websites are easy to maintain and improve. If your site is a disorganized haphazard mess, it causes you more work in the long run. And if you have a complex site, you need a lot of time to make sure all the parts work together. Starting simple and trying to maintain that simplicity can be helpful in the long run.

Designing Your Site

I f you've spent much time surfing the web, you've probably noticed some sites that are well designed and others that are not. The design of your site is important because it sets the stage for your content and has the potential to keep visitors from leaving your site too quickly and to keep them coming back. This is sometimes called sticky content because it keeps visitors stuck to your website. The design involves colors, fonts, images, and layout.

This chapter shows you how to make decisions about developing an effective design and where you can find some ideas that will help spark your design creativity.

I Can't Make a Website That Looks That Good!

If you're reading this book, you're probably not a professional web designer. Neither am I. But you don't need to be to create a well-designed website. You can learn from the work of others—those with great talent and ability who create true works of art (see Figure 4.1).

FIGURE 4.1

cork'd is a well-designed wine tasting site.

Most of the beautiful and well-designed sites out there were created by a staff that is well trained and well paid. Compared to these sites, your site will look unpolished and unprofessional. However, it's important to remember that this is a learning process and your budget is probably zero, so keep things in perspective. Learn from the sites that are well done and, most importantly, don't get discouraged! Have fun and be creative.

Content Before Design

If there is one core principle that guides all my website design, it's content before design. This means collecting the content for your website and then letting that guide and inform your design. For example, if you are building a website for your bowling team, consider the content first. Your team wants to have member profiles, a schedule, results from past matches, and the team logo. Let those things guide your design of the website.

Overall Design

To start, let's consider the overall design of your site. What mood do you want to evoke with your website—do you want it to be fun and bright or dark and brooding? Maybe you don't even know. The best place to start is by looking around at sites that are well designed.

Design Ideas

I am always looking for design ideas. When I find a site that is well designed, I *bookmark* it so that when I am beginning a new design, I can review it to get ideas for my own site.

I also look at the winners of design awards and web designers' sites. Because these sites are well designed, you can learn a lot from them.

Here are a few to consider:

Geek Speak

bookmark

Most browsers enable you to bookmark sites, which means you keep a record of a particular website so you can go back to it later. Check your browser's documentation to learn how to bookmark with your browser.

- Webby Awards (www.webbyawards.com)
- LevelTen Interactive (www.leveltendesign.com)
- Avenue A/Razorfish (www.avenuea-razorfish.com)

Central Image Design

One way to design your site is to use a central image and base your color scheme and other images off it. This works particularly well if you have something like a logo or photo to work from.

Colors

The web is a visual medium, so color is important. It invokes mood and can make one site dynamic and interesting and another bland and boring. Millions of colors are available to you, so let your creativity and personal style be your guide.

The Magic Four

If you go to your local newsstand and look at the colors used on magazines, you will most likely see the following dominant colors:

- Red
- Yellow
- Black
- White

These are the magic colors in advertising. If you are unsure about what colors to use, start with one of these. On the other hand, if you're looking for something different and want a color that matches certain images or other design elements of your site, you have a multitude of options.

Hex Color

When you are dealing with color on the Internet, you need to understand that roses are not "red" but "#FF0000." This is called hex color, and you have to get used to it when you're using color on the web. The strange notation is really three sets of numbers: FF, 00, and 00. (FF is actually a number in this case.)

Each two-digit number is a hexadecimal value of a much larger number. The three sets of numbers in a hex code represent red, green, and blue (often referred to as RGB). HTML tags use the hex number to define colors.

Each color (red, green, and blue) has 256 possible values, and the three of them together make all other colors. To determine the hex value for a number, you use a scientific calculator. For Windows, follow these steps:

1. Press the Windows key and R.
2. In the Run box, type `calc.exe`, and then click OK.
3. From the View menu, select Scientific (see Figure 4.2).
4. Type 214, and then click the Hex option.
5. The Hex value of 214, which is D6, is displayed. Many HTML tags and other applications use hexadecimal to describe colors.

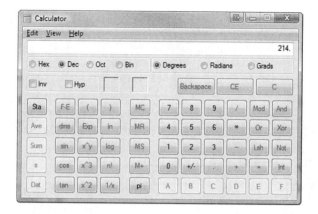

FIGURE 4.2

The scientific calculator.

As practice, find the RGB numbers of your favorite color and convert them to hexadecimal.

Color Schemes

A set of colors that complement each other is called a color scheme. These colors simply look good together and probably contain one of the four magic colors. A couple of tools on the web can help you match colors.

■ **Color Combos (www.colorcombos.com/)**—This website is all about creating color combinations for the web (see Figure 4.3). You can use it to pick existing color combinations, test combinations, and browse their color combination library.

■ **Color Palette Generator (www. degraeve.com/color-palette/)**—If you have a central image around which you want to build your website, all you need to do is load it into this website, and the tool determines the colors used in the picture (see Figure 4.4).

note If you find the perfect picture on the web, such as on flickr, and want to use it on your website, remember to get the owner's permission.

■ **ColorBlender (http://colorblender.com/)**—This tool enables you to create matching colors and a color palette based on a color you select. If you know the central color you want to use, this site gives you options to use with it.

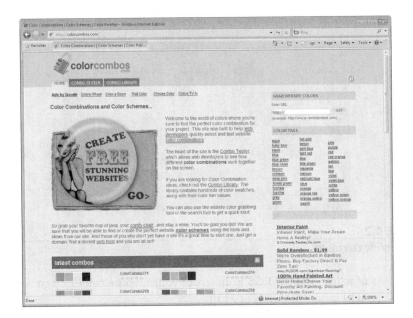

FIGURE 4.3

Color Combos is a site with many color tools.

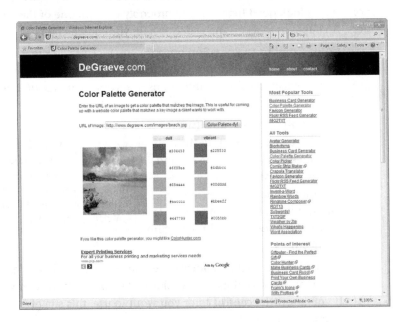

FIGURE 4.4

The Color Palette Generator finds the color palette used in an image.

■ **colrpickr (www.krazydad.com/colrpickr/)**—This site finds pictures on flickr that match the color you choose.

■ **COLOURlovers (www.colourlovers.com/)**—This is a website and community dedicated to color on websites (see Figure 4.5). These people take color seriously and have a lot of fun doing it. They also follow trends of web color. You can find some good color advice on this site.

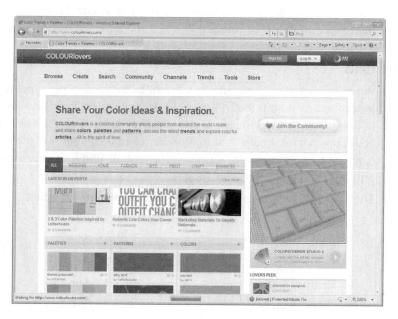

FIGURE 4.5
COLOURlovers is a colorful community.

Color Blindness

One thing to be wary of when working with color is that a portion of the population is color blind and might not be seeing website colors as you do. This is especially relevant with red, green, and blue. Try not to mix red, blue, and green text and red, blue, and green background. Text and background like this may prevent color blind people from seeing the text at all.

If you are color blind, make sure a person who is not color blind checks out the colors on your site.

The Colorblind Web Page filter (http://colorfilter.wickline.org/) can show you what your site looks like to a color blind person, so take the time to run your page through the filter. If you use this tool on some popular sites like cnn.com and huffingtonpost.com, you will see that the site is still easy to read and use.

Fonts

There is usually some amount of text on a web page. Some pages have little text, and others have a huge amount of text. This text can either be actual text or graphics that appear as text. To begin, I will deal with text as text and then move on to text as images.

System Fonts

When using text on a website, you might be inclined to use some type of fancy font. Avoid this if at all possible. Several system fonts have been created to display well on web pages. If you use a special font and the person viewing your page does not have that font on her computer, your text reverts back to a system font. Also, system fonts are different on Windows versus Apple computers. (Some things are never easy!)

The following are the default system fonts on Windows systems:

- Arial
- Book Antiqua
- Calisto MT
- Century Gothic
- Comic Sans MS
- Copperplate Gothic Bold
- Copperplate Gothic Light
- Courier
- Courier New
- Fixedsys
- Georgia
- Impact
- Lucida Console
- Lucida Handwriting Italic
- Lucida Sans Italic
- Lucida Sans Unicode
- Marlett
- Matisse ITC
- Modern
- MS Serif
- MS Sans Serif
- News Gothic MT
- OCR A Extended
- Small Fonts
- Symbol
- System
- Tempus Sans ITC
- Terminal
- Times New Roman
- Verdana
- Webdings
- Westminster
- Wingdings

The following are the default system fonts on Apple systems:

- AmericanTypewriter
- Andale Mono
- Apple Chancery
- Apple Symbols
- Arial
- Baskerville
- BigCaslon
- Brush Script
- Chalkboard
- Charcoal
- Cochin
- Comic Sans MS
- Copperplate
- Courier
- Courier New
- Didot
- Futura
- Gadget
- Geneva
- Georgia
- Gill Sans
- Helvetica
- Helvetica Neue
- Herculanum
- Hoefler Text
- Impact
- Marker Felt
- Optima
- Papyrus
- Skia
- Symbol
- Times New Roman
- Trebuchet MS
- Verdana
- Webdings
- Zapf Dingbats
- Zapfino

A good rule of thumb regarding fonts is not to specify fonts at all unless necessary. If you have to use a font, make sure it is a system font. Finally, if you need to use a font you know is not a system font, turn the text into an image.

Fonts as Images

When necessary, you can save text of a particular type as an image (see Figure 4.6). The problem with this is that the text is no longer selectable, and search engines cannot find it. Also, these images slow down your page's load time.

FIGURE 4.6

An example of fonts used in an image.

Fonts and Color

You can also color the text on your web page.

When dealing with text, try to use black text on a white background. Colored text and colored backgrounds can make things difficult to read. It is best to avoid using colored text and background, but at the very least, contrast the color of the text and the color of the background in such a way to make it easy to read. Some okay examples are green text on a black background or blue text on a white background.

Images

Images probably will be an important part of any design you create. However, it's a good idea not to include too many images in your web pages, because they can slow down the rate at which the pages download and visually overwhelm the pages. Try to find a few strong images that support your content well. I cover images and working with them in Chapter 11, "Working with Images."

Cascading Style Sheets

The best way to keep your web page's design consistent is to use a cascading style sheet (CSS). This acts as a guide for your web page to format certain elements in certain ways. If you want all your links to be red and underlined, you can set up an element in the CSS and control the formatting of all the links.

→   I cover how to set up and use CSS in Chapter 13, "Building a Site Using HTML."

Design Best Practices

There are no hard and fast rules in creating a design for a web page, but there are some best practices to help you avoid common mistakes. Remember to keep your design simple and consistent, and your site will look great.

Content Is King

More than anything, let your content guide you in the design of your site. If you are trying to sell helmets for motorcyclists and your website has no pictures of your helmets or people wearing your helmets, no one will come to your site again.

Put What Is New Front and Center

One common mistake of beginning web designers is making new content on their website inaccessible to visitors. Put anything new front and center. Also, tell your visitor it is new and your site is up to date. This is how your website will create return visitors.

Keep It Simple

Keep your design as simple as possible. You don't want a visually confusing or complex site that loses or overwhelms your visitors.

Don't Use Attention Grabbers

Resist the urge to use attention-grabbing design elements such as neon colors and blinking text. Like Times Square all lit up, attention grabbers can be overwhelming and off-putting to the visitor.

Be Consistent

Keep your colors, fonts, and images consistent. For example, if you use certain colors on one page of the site, use the same colors on the other pages. Also, if your organization has an established logo or color scheme, stay consistent with proven or already accepted design. You don't want to confuse your visitors.

4

Gathering Your Tools

No matter what you do, it's always important to have the right tools for the job. In this chapter, I want to show you the best web development tools you can get for absolutely free. By tools, I mean software utilities, or programs, that you can use to help create your website.

Now, I'm sure you're thinking that you can't get something for nothing. Well, I'll show you a bunch of graphics programs that are just as good as or better than commercial software, and they're 100% free! This is community-developed software that is open source, shared, and best of all, free of charge.

Web development tools come in many shapes and sizes. Some are programs you download to your computer, and others are websites you go to and use as programs.

Finding the Right Tools for the Job

You're probably wondering where you will find all these wonderful, free tools. I'm going to show you some websites where you can find and download excellent open-source utilities.

To begin, the best thing to do is to use a search engine to find a free or open-source alternative to what you are trying to find. For example, if I Google `Photoshop open source alternative`, I get several options, including the open-source graphics editor called GIMP. In this chapter, I do some of the legwork for you and give you some of my sources of information and recommended programs.

Tool Sites and Reviews

The following is a list of some great sites that list open-source software programs. These sites are excellent places to find the latest and greatest version of open-source software programs. They sort the utilities into categories and give short descriptions of the software so you can easily find what you're looking for. You can find almost anything here, especially free alternatives to other programs. Don't just look at the alternatives, though; sometimes open source creates programs that mainstream software companies have not thought up yet, such as podcasting and peer-to-peer utilities. The sites then give you links that go directly to the latest versions of the utilities where you can download them.

- **Open Source Windows**—www.opensourcewindows.org/
- **Open Source Mac**—www.opensourcemac.org/
- **Open Source as Alternative**—www.osalt.com/
- **The Top 50 Proprietary Programs That Drive You Crazy—and Their Open Source Alternatives**—http://whdb.com/2008/the-top-50-proprietary-programs-that-drive-you-crazy-and-their-open-source-alternatives/

Downloading New Software

Software tools and utilities fall into two categories: programs that you download and then install on your computer, and programs that reside on websites you access with your browser. Downloading software might be a new process for you, so the following instructions walk you through how to do this:

1. Find the site that has the files you want to download and install.

   When you go to an open-source utilities site, you are given information about the program and a link to download the software. Make sure you find the link for downloading the latest *stable version* of the software that is right for your operating system.

2. Click the download link. When you download files to your computer, they usually include instructions for how to install them. Take the time to read these instructions, because they can provide valuable information about how to install and run the program.

3. After you have downloaded the files, follow the instructions to install the program.

Geek Speak

stable or release version

The stable version of software is one that has been tested and is ready for limited release. In other words, the program is expected to do most of what it is expected to do. You might see software identified as "beta" or "alpha." This simply means the software is currently being developed. Almost all the open-source software you encounter is going to be in the middle of some development process. Essentially, it is constantly being updated and changed. The terms alpha and beta identify certain levels of stability. Alpha software is early in the process, and beta is a bit further on. You can expect some problems with alpha software and fewer with beta software.

Essential Tools

To create a website, you need certain tools. All the software listed in the following sections is free and open sourced. Each of the tools performs an important task for your website or enables you to create web pages and other content.

Operating Systems

To begin, you can use open source to run your whole computer. Normally, you would have the Apple or Microsoft

caution When downloading any software to your computer from the Internet, there is a possibility that bad things could happen. The software could install incorrectly or, worse, affect the existing files on your computer. On the other hand, the open-source community does a great job of policing itself, and downloading and installing open-source software usually is a painless process.

(Windows) operating systems running things on your computer, but there are open-source alternatives. Open-source operating systems have the benefit of being free and customizable but can be less stable and without much support. Using an open-source operating system can be risky. Not all programs work on open-source operating systems, and open source may make your whole computer unstable. This being said, open-source operating systems are a lot of fun and solve some of the problems that other operating systems have (not least of all is cost). I usually run one or more open-source operating systems on one of my older computers to see how stable it is before loading it onto one of my newer computers.

- **Linux (www.linux.org/)**—The granddaddy of open-source operating systems
- **Ubuntu (www.ubuntu.com/)**—Another robust stable open-source operating system
- **Qimo (www.qimo4kids.com/)**—A fun operating system for kids that you can run on almost any computer

Web Browsers

Having a good browser is one of the most essential tools in web design. You have to be familiar with all the ways people can see your web pages. These are some of the most stable, robust open-source applications on the web, and they are essential to your toolbox.

- **Firefox (www.firefox.com/)**—The best and most popular open-source browser.
- **Google Chrome (www.google.com/chrome)**—Google's browser has come a long way to be a real contender in the web browser market.

Office Suites

Although not directly related to web design, office suites are powerful collections of programs to help communicate, document, and calculate information. Listed here are some open-source alternatives to Microsoft Office.

- **OpenOffice**—www.openoffice.org
- **NeoOffice**—www.neooffice.org

File Transfer Protocol (FTP) Programs

FTP stands for File Transfer Protocol and is a fancy name for the software that enables you to easily transfer files between machines over the Internet. When uploading your website files to your web server, you need an FTP client—the program that does this for you. The more advanced features include queuing up multiple files and saving connection information and transfer reports.

Here are a few recommendations:

- **FileZilla (Windows, Linux, and Mac) (http://filezilla-project.org/)**— This open-source FTP client (see Figure 5.1) offers a full range of features (and running an application with "zilla" in the name is fun).

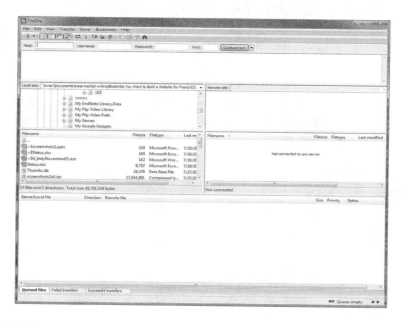

FIGURE 5.1

FileZilla enables you to move files to and from the Internet.

- **Fetch (Mac) (http://fetchsoftworks.com/)**—This FTP client is a free download with the cutest little dog mascot. It's a favorite of Mac users.
- **Cyberduck (Mac) (http://cyberduck.ch/)**—A great little multifunctional, free, open-source FTP client that comes in several languages.

- **OneButton FTP (Mac) (http://onebutton.org/)**—A simple free FTP program geared to Mac users with low technical skills who just want to move files as easily as possible.

- **Net2ftp (www.net2ftp.com/)**—A free website FTP client that requires no download to your machine and works on several platforms with different browsers.

Text Editor

When building websites, you must be able to edit text files, including Hypertext Markup Language (HTML) files or script files. A text file is simply a file with words and numbers and no formatting. Here are some of the better text editors:

- **Notepad (Windows)**—The standard text editor that comes with all versions of Windows

- **Notepad ++ (Windows, Linux) (http://notepad-plus.sourceforge.net/uk/site.htm)**—An excellent free Notepad alternative that has many excellent features, such as line numbers and text checking (see Figure 5.2)

FIGURE 5.2

A program such as Notepad ++ is essential when editing text files.

- **TextWrangler (Mac) (www.barebones.com/products/textwrangler/index.shtml)**—An excellent text editor for the Mac
- **XEmacs (Windows, Linux, UNIX) (www.xemacs.org/index.html)**—A more technically oriented text editor with some advanced features

Graphics Editors

A graphics editor enables you to create, edit, and format graphics files. This utility is essential in making your website look amazing, which it does by enabling you to manipulate photos, drawings, or computer art. You might want to change an existing graphic or create something new. This utility allows for unlimited creativity. In addition, a graphics editor makes it possible to change the size and file type of graphics, making your web page load quickly and efficiently.

Here are some recommended graphics editors:

- **GIMP (Windows, Mac, Linux) (www.gimp.org/)**—This is the best and most popular open-source image manipulation utility. It has many features, is easy to use, and you can't beat the price (FREE!).
- **Inkscape (Windows, Mac, Linux) (http://inkscape.org/)**—This is a free open-source drawing program. If the artistic urge comes over you, run this program to bring your vision into digital reality. It is similar to Adobe Illustrator.
- **Paint.Net (Windows) (www.getpaint.net/)**—This is an open-source photo-editing software package originally designed by students. It has grown into a large-scale open-source software project.
- **Seashore (Mac OS X) (http://seashore.sourceforge.net/)**—This is a version of GIMP for a specific version of the Mac OS X operating system.

HTML Editors

HTML editors are used to create and edit web pages. Some of them use a graphical user interface (GUI), and others are simpler and only allow you to edit the text of the HTML file.

If you need to edit the look of a web page or the code behind it, use an HTML editor. An editor gives you shortcuts (such as preformatted tags and auto closing tags) and formats the pages for you so that your life is a whole lot easier.

The following are some recommended HTML editors:

- **KompoZer (Windows, Mac, Linux) (www.kompozer.net/)**—A full-featured multiplatform what you see is what you get (WYSIWYG) editor for web pages and site management. This program is easy to install and use.

- **Quanta Plus (Windows, Linux) (http://quanta.kdewebdev.org/)**—A feature-rich HTML editor. It has such a range of features that it can be overwhelming to newer users, so this is for technically minded folks.

- **Bluefish (Windows, Mac, Linux) (http://bluefish.openoffice.nl/)**—A decent HTML editor with the capability to write websites and scripts in several languages.

- **SeaMonkey (Windows, Mac, Linux) (www.seamonkey-project.org/)**—This tool is a bit different. Along with being a tool for emailing, reading newsgroups, chatting, and web browsing, it is a full-featured HTML editing tool (see Figure 5.3). Brought to you by the folks who make Firefox, this is a useful tool.

- **WaveMaker (Mac) (www.wavemaker.com/downloads/)**—A development tool for both web and cloud applications.

FIGURE 5.3

SeaMonkey is a multifunction tool.

- **OpenLaszlo (Windows, Mac, Linux) (www.openlaszlo.org/)**—This tool is for the advanced development of web applications. Use it to add some programming and interaction to your site rather than just giving out information. It's not for everyone, but it's worth a look.

- **CSSED (Windows, Linux) (http://cssed.sourceforge.net/)**—A full-featured and expandable cascading style sheets (CSS) editing tool. (For more information on how to use CSS, look at Chapter 4, "Designing Your Site.") This is for the more technically minded website developer. If you have mastered some other tools, you might want to give this one a try.

Sound Recorders

If you want to use audio on your website, you might need a sound recording program. Here's a popular one to consider:

- **Audacity (Windows, Mac, Linux) (http://audacity.sourceforge. net/)**—If your website needs sound and you need to edit some raw sound files, this tool lets you record, play, and edit sound files.

Video Editing

The web is filled with more and more video every day. A few years ago, adding video to a website was difficult, slow, and expensive. Now video is everywhere on the web. With more and more people using broadband, video is common on websites. These tools help you capture, edit, and render video:

- **Blender (Windows, Mac, Linux) (www.blender.org/)**—The premier open-source video-editing tool.

- **Cinelerra-CV (Linux) (http://cinelerra.org/)**—A great tool, but only available for use on a Linux operating system.

Advanced Tools

If you think you have the skills for more advanced web development tools, read on. Programs with more features are more difficult to learn, install, and use. Here are some recommendations:

- **Nvudev (Windows, Mac, Linux) (http://nvudev.com/index.php)**—A more complex, less polished version of KompoZer. This is hot off the presses, so it might have more bugs than some of the other options listed here.

- **phpMyAdmin (Web Utility) (www.phpmyadmin.net/)**—If you are using a MySQL database, you have to use this tool. It is the most full-featured, easy-to-use front end to a MySQL database there is.
- **EasyPHP (Web Utility) (www.easyphp.org/)**—An excellent tool for development and upkeep of PHP scripts that dynamically create web pages.

The Future of Free Web Tools

All the tools discussed in this chapter are free. Over the past decade and a half we have seen more and more free software being made available online. In that time, the quality of this software has also risen. This makes using free web software for your project a viable option.

Open-source software is being used more and more each day. New tools with new and better features constantly arrive on the scene. The best yet is the tool that you don't even know you need that some open-source developer is working on right now. Keep looking, and enjoy the fruits of so many people's labor.

5

Moving Files to and from the Internet

One of the most common questions people have when they start to build their own websites is how to transfer the files to the Internet. This chapter shows you that it's easier than you think.

The simplest way to understand putting your files on the Internet is to realize all you are doing is moving files from one computer to another. If you have moved files between computers at home or work, you have essentially done everything you need to do to move files to the Internet.

Moving files from the Internet to your computer is called downloading. When you are moving files from your computer to the Internet you are uploading them.

The best way to transfer files to and from the Internet is by using File Transfer Protocol (FTP). Several FTP programs are outlined in Chapter 5, "Gathering Your Tools." An FTP program enables you to connect to a server on the Internet that allows FTP connections. When you're connected to an FTP server, you can move files to and from that server. This chapter tells you how to use those programs to actually move your files.

Storing Your Files

Before you start thinking about moving your files to and from the Internet, it's important to take some time to organize your files on your own computer. Keeping things organized is going to make it easier to find things and ensures fewer errors when moving files. This section covers some best practices for your file storage and introduces you to a more efficient way of storing files.

A common problem with new web developers is that they often reference files incorrectly. This can cause all sorts of problems and can drive you nuts if you don't organize your files. A common example of this is when you reference images in a web page on your computer and not the web server. If you look at the HTML code and see a reference like C:\users\Tom\Webpagepics\cat.jpg, the web server can't find that file, so it returns an error.

Naming Files

One question you'll probably ask when you create files to use on your website is, "What should I name this file?" You really can name your files just about anything, but here are a few simple rules you should follow.

Make the Names Simple

Try to keep your names as simple as possible and be as descriptive as possible. The description might be the file's purpose and dimensions. For example, instead of calling a graphics file picture01.jpg, maybe try logo125x125.jpg. This way you know the file is a logo, and you know its size without ever having to open it.

Always Use Lowercase

With some servers and web hosts, the case of a file you are referring to needs to be very specific. If a server has the file named in uppercase LOGO.gif and you make a reference in HTML to the file using lowercase, logo.gif, the server might not know you mean the same file.

By keeping all your filenames lowercase, you ensure you are always going to have clean references.

Don't Use Spaces

Using spaces in a filename is not a good idea. When a browser encounters a space in an HTML filename, it fills it in with %20. So, www.bobshouseofpancakes.com/our menu.html

becomes

www.bobshouseofpancakes.com/our%20menu.html

Because this is not the exact name of your page, referring to it this way makes the page impossible for your browser to find. You don't have this problem if your filenames have no spaces.

If you need to use a space, one solution is to use an underscore, which is the character above the subtraction sign/hyphen (-) on most computers. Usually, you press the subtraction/hyphen key and Shift at the same time. This changes the filename reallylongconfusingfilename.html to really_long_confusing_file_name.html. The filename is easier to read, and with no spaces you don't run the risk of a bad HTML address.

Keep All Your Web Files in One Place

This might seem like a simple thing, but storing your files in one place on your hard drive is often overlooked. Keeping your HTML files, images, and scripts straight on your computer is going to make your life much easier in the long run. This is especially true if you are working on more than one website at once.

Have an Organizational Structure

After you have all your files in one place, the next thing you want to do is organize them. This makes it easier for you to find what you are looking for and to store new files. You can do this in any number of ways, but when I am working on multiple websites, I use folders to store all the pieces of one website in one place (see Figure 6.1). Within the website folder, I have folders for HTML files, graphics, and multimedia scripts. By creating the same directory structure each time, I find things more easily and have fewer reference errors in my code.

Website folder

Images folder

Scripts folder

Multimedia folder

HTML files

6

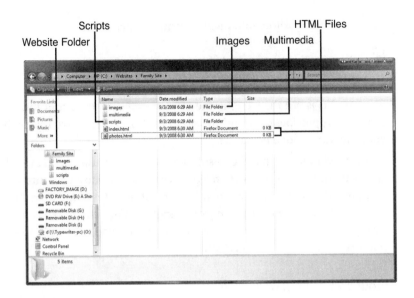

FIGURE 6.1
An example of a file storage structure.

Use a Version Control System

If you are building multiple websites or are collaborating on one with a lot of people, you might want to consider version control systems. These store, keep track of, and monitor who is using files for your projects and ensure that you don't accidentally overwrite changes another person has made. Subversion is a free open source version control system that thousands of software developers use.

If you are interested, you can learn more at the following websites:

- **A Visual Guide to Version Control**—http://betterexplained.com/articles/a-visual-guide-to-version-control
- **Revision Control**—http://en.wikipedia.org/wiki/Revision_control
- **Subversion**—http://subversion.apache.org

Uploading Files to the Internet

After your website is finished and ready to go live, you need to move the files onto a computer (your web server) on which you are connected to the Internet. To do this, you connect to a server that allows FTP connections. Most often, your web server will allow FTP connections.

To do this, you need an FTP program like those described in Chapter 5. I am going to use Filezilla for these examples, but any FTP program should be able to move files to and from your FTP server.

Logging In

Before you start, you need some information that your host provider will give you, including the name of the FTP server to which you want to connect, the username, and your password. You might have had to define your username and password when you signed on to the hosting service, but you might need to check with them to make sure the same username and password are what you use for your FTP login information.

After you have this information, log in to the server. The FTP program window has two sides. One side shows the files on your computer, and the other side shows the files on the web host's computer.

To log in to an FTP server, do this:

1. In the Host field, enter your hostname.
2. Enter your username and password in the correct fields.
3. Unless your host provider told you to use a specific port, leave the Port field blank.
4. Click the Quickconnect button.

You are now connected to the FTP server at your host (see Figure 6.2).

Adding New Files

After you have connected to an FTP server, all you need to do is drag the files from your computer to the server. This does not delete the files from your computer but places a copy on the FTP server.

Changing Existing Files

If you try to copy a file that already exists on the FTP server, the FTP program alerts you to this. You are given the choice to overwrite the file or cancel the transfer request (see Figure 6.3). Be careful when doing this, because you don't want to overwrite the wrong files.

note When in doubt, cancel a change to overwrite a file. That way you don't accidentally overwrite something.

6

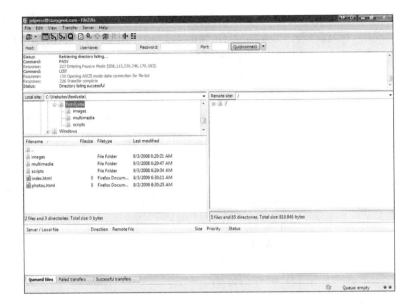

FIGURE 6.2

FileZilla connected to a server.

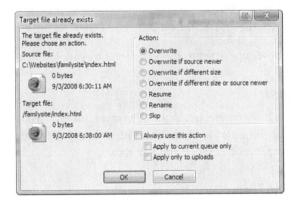

FIGURE 6.3

This window lets you overwrite the file or cancel transferring it.

Downloading Files from an FTP Server

What happens if you find a file on the Internet and want to download it? If you have FTP access to the server that stores the file you are looking for, you just need to connect to the server and do the reverse of the upload process.

One File or Many

When you download files from the Internet, sometimes you might be downloading one file and other times it might be a bunch of files combined into one. Both types download the same way, but when you download a group of files, you might have to do some extra things, such as run them or unzip them to get the individual files unpacked to your computer. What you need to do for different file types is covered in the next section.

Downloading from a Browser

Most browsers make it easy for you to download files; simply click the hyperlink to the file or use a submenu (such as a right-click menu) to download it. This works similar to FTP in that you are downloading a copy of the file onto your computer. Downloading a file from the Internet doesn't affect the file on the Internet.

Types of Download Files

Depending on the file and your operating system, downloads come in a few different types of files. Some of these files are easy to deal with, whereas others require special programs.

Files usually have two parts: the name of the file and a suffix that is the file extension. The file extension comes after the period (.) in the filename. The file extension tells you the type of file. It also tells the operating system what program to use to open it by default. So, for example, logo.bmp is a file named "logo" that is of the "BMP" or bitmap type.

The following sections describe some common file types and their uses.

> **note** If a file you are downloading has no extension or you are unfamiliar with the file extension, take the safe route and investigate the file extension before downloading it to your computer. This site lists hundreds of file extensions in alphabetical order:
>
> http://filext.com/alphalist.php?extstart=^A

Image Files (GIF, JPG, TIFF, BMP)

Graphics files don't require anything special to be done to them after they are downloaded, but you must have a graphics program to view and edit them. These days, most operating systems can deal with these files and show them to you, but you might run into a file that doesn't open right away. The open source graphics program GIMP (www.gimp.org/) should open anything you need.

EXE (Windows)

This is the extension used for self-contained executable files, which are files that run on their own when clicked. In Windows, all you need to do is double-click the downloaded file, and it begins to run.

> **caution** Be careful with these files—harmful files that could hurt your machine may be stored within executable files. Run only files that you download from a trusted source.

ZIP

A zip file compresses one or several files into one smaller file. This new, smaller file contains the files and maintains the file structure when unpacked. Most operating systems allow you to double-click these files to open them (see Figure 6.4).

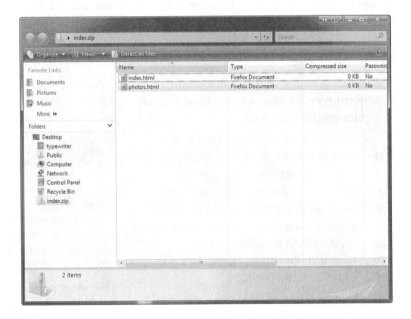

FIGURE 6.4
The contents of a zip file.

DMG (Mac)

This is basically the Mac version of the executable file. When you download a file like this to your Mac, just double-click it to run it.

ISO

This is a special type of compressed file that takes the entirety of a CD or DVD and puts it into one file. You need a special program that can unpack these large files and let you interact with the contents.

Best Practices for Downloading Files

Like the files you use to build your website, keeping your downloads organized is essential. Organization allows you to find files you are looking for and conserve space. Here are some best practices for downloading files:

- **Use a virus scanner on all downloads**—The Internet is full of excellent wonderful people but there are a few bad apples. Make sure you scan any download for viruses before you open it on your system.

- **Keep all your downloads in one place**—When you are downloading a lot of files, you need to keep them in one place so you can find them after you have downloaded them. I use a folder called Downloads where all my browsers put downloads.

- **Don't download to your desktop**—One place where you should not download files is your desktop. This is just going to clutter up your desktop and make it difficult to find anything.

- **Delete large package files after they are unpacked**—If you are downloading large files, such as ISO files, you should delete the file after you have unpacked it. You don't want to eat up all your hard drive space with files you use only once.

6

Website Building Basics

Elements of a Website

Before you jump into building your website, you need to understand its parts. I covered the definitions of a web page and a website earlier in this book, but these definitions need to be expanded if we are going to discuss building elements of web pages and websites.

This chapter covers what makes good content of websites, the parts of a web page, and the parts of a website. Finally, it covers web advertising and whether it has a place on your website.

Content

Content is the meat of your website, and it's the reason people come to it. If you don't have excellent, unique content, people have no reason to type in your URL or click on a link that leads to your site.

This section covers some best practices for developing your website content.

Content Best Practices

The subject of your content is really up to you, but there are some best practices for any content.

- **Content should be focused**—Your web content should have a point and focus on that point. Nothing puts off visitors like unfocused content. A website for antique typewriters should not have pictures of your dog's new pups on the front page. Define what you are going to talk about on your website, and stick to it.

- **Content should be personal**—If at all possible, make your content personal. You have personality, and I for one am interested in what you have to say. In fact, lots of people will be interested in what you have to say. No one has had the same experiences as you, so your content is unique. If your site is a business site, inject the personality of the business into your content. A site for a party clown company should look different from a financial advisor's site.

- **Content should be high quality**—Take pride in what you are putting out there. Make sure your content is written well and is free of mistakes. Provide the best site you can to your visitors.

- **Content should be unique**—Don't just be a repeater; be an innovator. Even if you are reposting what someone else has posted, tell us what you think of it; give us your take. The Internet Movie Database (see Figure 7.1) has succeeded because of its unique content.

- **Content should be appropriate to the audience**—Think of your audience when you are creating your content. What does your audience expect and want out of the content of your site? If you are creating a website for preschool kids, you would not use university-level language.

7

FIGURE 7.1

The Internet Movie Database has some of the best content on the Internet.

Content Standards

You can't control who visits your website. It could be your boss, your grandmother, or the eight-year-old kid who lives across the street. Those people might have different standards of what is appropriate than you do. I am not going to tell you to censor your content, but be aware it can be viewed by a wide range of people. If your site has some "risky" content that is of a more mature nature (things like language, jokes, or images)—the kind you don't want your grandmother to see—you might want to consider clearly labeling that content to warn off those who would be offended by it.

Geek Speak

NSFW

You might hear people in emails or on blogs referring to content as NSFW. This means Not Safe For Work. The idea is that this is not the kind of content that you should be viewing at work but is better viewed at home. This would include adult images or content. If you are unsure whether your content falls into this area, you might want to label it NSFW.

7

Parts of a Web Page

This section covers some of the standard parts of a web page design. These parts are different from content. They provide containers for your content. Not every web page has all these elements, but a good web page has most of them.

Title

The title of a web page appears in the title bar of the browser displaying your web page. It might seem like something to overlook, but it can be important. This is how your page is identified when visitors are scanning their application titles in the taskbar or the Dashboard. When a browser is minimized or your web page appears in a tab, the title appears in the tab or in your Windows program bar (see Figure 7.2).

The title is defined by an HTML tag in your code. For more information on using the title tag, see Chapter 10, "HTML 101."

FIGURE 7.2

Google Calendar's title shows up at the top of my browser and in its tab.

Header

The header of a web page is the area that spans the top of the page. There is no set size to this, but a common convention dictates that the header be no more than a quarter of the total page length and span the width of the page. A header can contain site title information and navigational elements (see Figure 7.3). A header can also be used over and over again on each page to increase website consistency. If you have one consistent header file for all your pages you only need to change that file once to update the entire site.

Body

The body is the main part of your web page. The majority of your content goes in the body of the page. There are no real standards for the body of a web page, but keep in mind that your content should be visually easy to read (see Figure 7.4). For instance, if the body of a web page spans all the way across the browser, it might be harder to read on some monitors.

FIGURE 7.3
The header part of the Twitter.com page.

FIGURE 7.4
The body of the IBM website.

Footer

Mirroring the header is the footer. It spans the bottom part of the page and again can be used for informational or navigational elements (see Figure 7.5). Also, like the header, it is good to replicate this on each page of the website to maintain consistency. If you have one consistent footer file for all your pages you only need to change that file once to update the entire site. This is also a common area for contact information.

Sidebars

Along the sides of the body content area, you may want to add sidebars. These are columns of website content that have more height than width. Like the header and footer, these sidebars can contain just about anything, but they are good for search fields and navigational elements (see Figure 7.6).

FIGURE 7.5

The footer of the Apple.com website.

FIGURE 7.6

This website has sidebars on either side of the body content.

Navigational Elements

Different parts of your web page may include navigational elements. These are important things to put on every web page. The navigational elements are the links to the other pages on the website. Without navigational elements, a visitor to your website can't get around and access all your content.

Your navigational elements can be text, buttons, or a menu. There is no set format for how your navigational elements should look, but they should be complete and consistent (see Figure 7.7). Here are the basic requirements for your navigational elements:

- **Complete**—Make sure all the pages on your site are accessible from all other pages on your site. Each site should have some navigational element in the collection of navigational elements that should appear on each page.

- **Consistency**—The navigational elements should appear in the same spot and contain the same links on every page. If you choose to disable the link of the page, make sure you do this consistently for each page.

- **Easy to read**—The navigational elements you use should be easy to read and understand. No one likes only hoping that a clicked link leads to the desired content.

- **Easy to find**—Don't hide your navigational elements on your web page. They should be easy to find and at the same place on each page.

FIGURE 7.7
This site has excellent navigational elements.

Parts of a Website

Just as there are parts of a web page, there are parts to a website. Not every website has all these parts, but you should be aware of them and determine whether your website needs them.

Home Page

This is the most important part of your website. I cannot stress this enough. The home page is the page that first loads when your website URL is entered in any browser.

When your URL is typed into a browser, the browser connects to your web server and requests your home page. By default, the web server sends the page index.htm or index.html to the browser. This is one convention that makes the web work so well.

The home page is where you make your first impression to your visitors, so make sure you are putting your best foot forward. The home page should also be your website's center point. Put your best and latest content on your home page (see Figure 7.8). People are not going to hang out at your website unless you make your home page the best part.

FIGURE 7.8

An example of a home page.

Content Pages

Your website is going to contain its own unique content pages (product pages, picture pages, and that sort of thing), but I have listed here a couple of examples of standard content pages.

About Me Page

This page is pretty self-explanatory from the title. You should cover who you are and why you have created the website. Make sure the information is clear, complete, and up to date.

Frequently Asked Questions

This is a list of frequently asked questions and answers (FAQ) about the purpose or content of your website (see Figure 7.9). This list should include questions and answers about your products or services or anything else that you think your visitors will ask on a frequent basis. This list will allow people to find information they need in a quick and organized way. Keep your FAQ up to date, and add to it often.

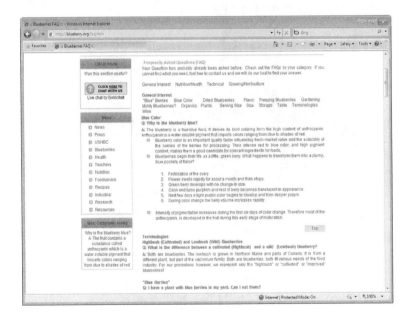

FIGURE 7.9

An example of an excellent website FAQ.

Contact Information

Adding your contact information to your website allows people to contact you with comments and questions about your website. This may include your name, address, phone number, and email address.

caution Be aware that spammers can find and use your contact information. One way around this is to write your email address in words so that spam bots can't find it. For example, instead of mark@markwbell.com, try using mark at markwbell dot com.

Web Advertising

One way you can subsidize your website is by selling advertising space there. First, this is not a quick way to become filthy rich. Making any profit through web advertising is difficult and unlikely to happen, but you might be able to subsidize part of your website costs.

note This is a simple overview of web advertising. If you enter into any business relationship with others (especially over the Internet), be sure to practice due diligence.

Before you go searching for advertisers for your website, you might want to spend your time and energy on making your website the best it can be and attract advertisers that way.

Banner Ads

Banner ads are advertisements that appear at different places on your website and allow people to click on the ad and go to an advertiser's site. You are essentially being paid to provide a link to another website.

Animated Ads

Over the past few years, there has been a trend in website advertising to create animated or interactive ads to attract the attention of website visitors. Unfortunately, these tend to have the opposite effects and just annoy visitors. My advice here is to take the high road and not use these ads on your website.

7

Google AdSense

One of the newer options for using ads on your website is to use the Google AdSense service (https://www.google.com/adsense/; see Figure 7.10). This service places text ads on your website, based on your content, and pays you a very small amount for them.

FIGURE 7.10
The Google AdSense web page.

These ads are less intrusive than attention-grabbing animated banner ads, but you have no control over what is displayed or when. Say you have a site based on your stamp collecting hobby. Google AdSense scans your page for keywords and display ads based on those keywords (see Figure 7.11). Google has specific rules and regulations with AdSense, so be sure to read the fine print before signing up with the service.

FIGURE 7.11

Google AdSense being used on a website.

Using Existing Websites

Most of you picked up this book because you want to build your own website. But some of you just want to create a web presence and are not interested in building an entire website. If you're one of the latter, you're in luck. There are websites (MySpace.com, Facebook.com, Flickr.com) that allow you to create a profile, meet other people, share pictures, and get information—all without having to mess with site planning, web servers, Hypertext Markup Language (HTML), or navigation.

In their most advanced form, these sites offer blogs, photo albums, email features, and instant messengers, all under the roof of one website.

If you already have an account on one of these websites but need something more, you probably need your own website. If you are unsure, sign up for these sites and see whether it fulfills your needs.

One of the benefits of this type of website is that it allows you to promote your website to other people. I am a member of all of these websites, and when I publish a new blog entry or am doing a speaking engagement, I use these sites to promote these events.

Social Networking Sites

Social networks have been around since the beginning of people. Social network websites started popping up on the Internet in 2002. Since their appearance, social network sites have become a dominant type of website, even featured on the cover of *Time* magazine. Most people have heard of these sites, and millions of people have accounts on them.

A social network site enables you to create a profile, connect with other people, and share your pictures and views.

A social network profile is like a home page about you. It contains information about you (as much or as little as you provide) and acts as a central point for the other social network site features.

Social networking might be seen as something that is for young people, but more people of all ages and backgrounds are using social networks.

This section covers three of the biggest social networks and explains how to sign up, create a profile, and connect with others. If you are already a member of any of these sites, you should review that particular section to make sure you are getting the most out of your social network experience.

> **caution** The instructions and features of these sites are subject to change with little notice, so you might find some differences between what you see on your screen and what you read here.

MySpace

MySpace (www.myspace.com) began in 2003 and grew out of an early Internet company named eUniverse. MySpace has all the standard features of a social network site and some other features that are similar to sites that allow you to build websites. It has millions of people and is one of the most popular websites on the Internet. By 2005, MySpace had become so popular that the media conglomerate News Corporation purchased it for $580 million.

This section covers the basics of using MySpace and some of its more website-like features.

> **caution** As with any account information, keep it confidential. Sharing this information enables those who know it to make changes to your MySpace account.

Creating an Account

Before you can create your MySpace profile, you have to have a MySpace account. This allows you to log in and authenticate who you are.

1. Open a browser and go to MySpace.com (see Figure 8.1).

FIGURE 8.1

The MySpace.com website.

2. Click the Sign Up button. This takes you to the MySpace.com Join MySpace Here page (see Figure 8.2). This page asks you to enter information about yourself so that MySpace can create an account for you.

> **note** If you are a musician, comedian, or filmmaker, MySpace.com has special sign-up areas for you. On this page, you will find links to these account creation pages.

3. Enter your information in the required fields. This information is not displayed in your profile unless you allow it.

4. Click the Terms of Use link and carefully read the terms of service (if you have nothing better to do).

FIGURE 8.2

The MySpace account creation page.

5. Click the Sign-Up button. After your account is created, MySpace allows you to invite some of your friends.

6. Click the confirmation link in the email you receive.

7. Add any bands and artists you might like to add to your friends list. When you're finished adding them, click Continue.

8. Upload a picture for your profile (see Figure 8.3).

9. If you'd like to affiliate your school so you can connect to classmates, click Continue.

10. Your profile is then displayed (see Figure 8.4).

> **note** Don't be that person who sends out tons of invites to people you barely know. Those people are no fun and never get invited to parties. If you want someone to be on your social network page, make sure you know that person well.

FIGURE 8.3

The Upload Photos page.

FIGURE 8.4

Your profile on MySpace.com.

Customizing Your Profile

After you have created a profile, you can add all sorts of information about yourself. Remember, anyone coming to MySpace looking for you can see this information, so do not include personal information such as your address and phone numbers.

1. To edit your profile, click the Edit Profile link on your profile. This displays the Edit Profile page (see Figure 8.5).

2. After you have edited your profile, click the Save Changes button.

FIGURE 8.5

The Edit Profile page on MySpace.com.

Connecting with Other Users

MySpace offers you a number of ways to connect with other users. You can search for users, email them, and even instant message other people on MySpace.com.

■ **Search and browsing**—MySpace enables you to search and browse (see Figure 8.6) other users by name, email address, age, gender, location, education, or level of interest.

FIGURE 8.6

The Browse Users page on MySpace.com.

- **Email**—MySpace offers a fully functional internal email system that also manages your messages, friend requests, and other connections.

- **Instant messaging**—MySpace enables you to download an instant messaging program that lists all your MySpace friends without requiring that you log on to MySpace.

Website Features

MySpace has several website-like features (blog, picture pages, calendar, and forums) that may be everything you need. You may already be using MySpace but not taking advantage of all these features. Try some of them; they can be a lot of fun!

- **Comments**—If you like someone's profile or want to send someone a public message, you can leave a comment on that person's profile. Remember that anyone visiting that person's profile page can see these comments.

- **Blog**—You can set up your own blog on MySpace and post entries that include text, images, and videos. You can also sign up to follow other people's blogs.

8

- **Photo Gallery**—MySpace is full of pictures. You can have hundreds of pictures on your account that are viewable by the public or just your friends. These pictures can also be collected into photo albums to keep them organized.

- **Applications**—MySpace now enables you to create and attach applications to your profile. For more information on MySpace applications, consult the MySpace Developer Platform community site (see Figure 8.7) (http://developer.myspace.com/community/).

- **Calendar**—If someone you follow on MySpace is holding events, the Calendar allows you to keep track of what is happening.

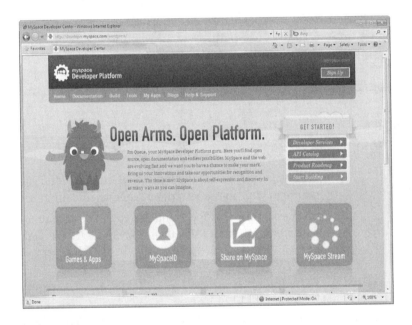

FIGURE 8.7
The MySpace Developer Platform community site.

Facebook

Mark Zuckerberg created Facebook in 2004 as a way to connect to people in his dorm at Harvard University. It quickly expanded to other universities and high schools. Originally, you had to have an email address associated with an educational institution to use Facebook, but in 2006 Facebook was opened to all users and has grown steadily ever since. Like MySpace, Facebook has millions of users.

This section covers the basics of using Facebook and some of the more website-like features.

Creating an Account

Before you can create your Facebook profile, you have to have a Facebook account. This enables you to log in and authenticate who you are.

> **caution** As with any account information, keep it confidential. Sharing this information enables those who know it to make changes to your Facebook account.

1. Open a browser and go to www.facebook.com (see Figure 8.8).

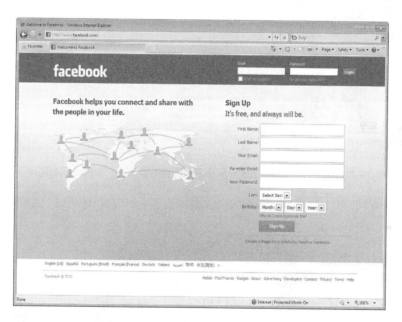

FIGURE 8.8

The Facebook.com website.

2. Enter the information you need to create an account on Facebook.

3. Click Sign Up.

4. Confirm your email address.

5. Search through your email contacts for other Facebook users and to invite people to Facebook (see Figure 8.9).

6. Enter information for your Facebook profile.

8

FIGURE 8.9
Use this page to find your friends that might already be on Facebook.

7. Your Facebook page is then displayed (see Figure 8.10).

FIGURE 8.10
My profile on Facebook.

Customizing Your Profile

After you have created a profile, you can add all sorts of information about yourself. Remember: Anyone coming to Facebook looking for you can see this information, so don't include personal information.

1. To edit your profile, click the Edit Profile link on your profile. This displays the profile page.

2. Click the Edit Information button to edit your profile (see Figure 8.11).

3. After you have edited your profile, click the Save Changes button.

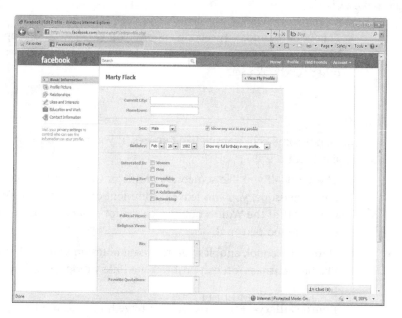

FIGURE 8.11

The Edit Profile page on Facebook.

Connecting with Other Users

Facebook offers you a number of ways to connect with other users. You can email users, chat with them, and join groups.

■ **Email**—Facebook offers a fully functional internal email system that also manages your messages, friend requests, and other connections.

■ **Facebook Chat**—Facebook enables you to chat with other Facebook users from the Facebook page (see Figure 8.12).

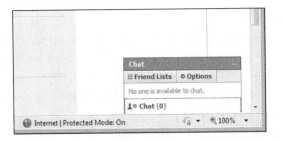

FIGURE 8.12

Using Facebook Chat.

■ **Facebook Groups**—Facebook enables you to connect to people with like interests. Remember: When you join a group, it becomes visible to other Facebook users.

Website Features

Facebook has some cool website-like features. If you're not already using them, give them a try!

■ **The Wall**—If you like someone's profile or want to send someone a public message, you can leave a comment on that person's Wall. Keep in mind that the Wall is public viewing for others, though; don't post anything too personal.

■ **Notes**—Facebook enables you to create notes on your profile that are like blog entries. You can post website links or videos within these notes.

■ **Photo Gallery**—Facebook lets you have hundreds of pictures on your page that the public can view. You can annotate these pictures and collect them into photo albums.

■ **Applications**—Facebook started the application craze that MySpace followed. For more information on Facebook applications, consult the Facebook Developers website at http://developers.facebook.com/. See Figure 8.13.

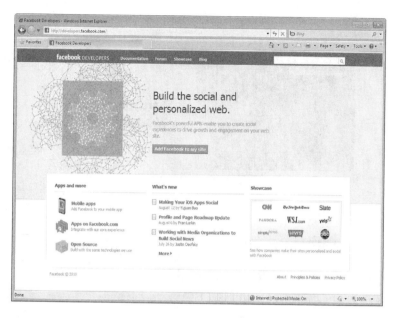

FIGURE 8.13

The Facebook Developers website.

Other Web 2.0 Sites

Web 2.0 is a fancy name for websites that allow you to interact with other people through your web browser. Facebook and MySpace let you connect to your friends. Other sites allow you to connect through photos and website links. This section covers some examples of Web 2.0 sites.

Social networks are not the only sites on the Internet that are useful for web development or promotion. Other Web 2.0 websites enable you to share pictures, links, and microblogs. (You'll read about those in a minute.) This section covers a few of these.

Flickr

Flickr (www.flickr.com) is the largest photo-sharing website in the world (see Figure 8.14). It enables you to create a profile, store your pictures, look at everyone else's public pictures, secure your personal pictures to only family and friends, and share your pictures with groups of other people. The site is full of amazing and fun features, so look around and play!

FIGURE 8.14
Flickr.com has some of the best photos on the Internet.

Twitter

You might have just gotten a handle on what blogging is, and along comes *microblogging*. This is blogging with only 140 characters in a mixture of chat room, blog, and constant news feed. Although not for everyone (you might not care when your friends are going to the grocery store), it can become wonderfully addictive. Twitter (Twitter.com) is currently the most popular microblogging site. I use it to promote my blog posts and my speaking engagements and share things I find that I like.

Since the first edition of *Build a Website for Free* in 2009, Twitter has really taken off. It has become part of international events, celebrity culture, and everyday life for millions of people all over the world. Recently, Twitter launched a Tweet button (see Figure 8.15). This button allows you to put code on your website that, when pressed, enables the visitor to automatically tweet about your website.

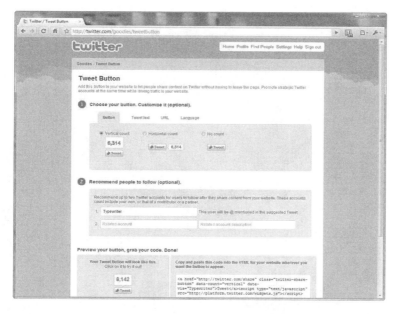

FIGURE 8.15

The new Twitter button page with everything you need to add it to your website.

Delicious.com

This website (www.delicious.com) might seem simple at first, but it offers a way to store and organize your bookmarks (by tagging) and allows you to share them with others, thereby creating connections you might never have thought of. It's a must for anyone doing research on the web or for anyone who has lost that great website's address.

Web Page Services

Maybe you still are not sure whether you need a full-blown website with your own web server, but you know you want more than the websites covered in the previous chapter have to offer.

Fortunately, there are a lot of people like you who want most of the functionality of a website but don't want the hassle of advanced functionality and maintenance complexity and lack the necessary technical knowledge. There is a type of website creation tool just for this group of people, commonly called web page services.

These services enable users to create websites using just their web browser (see Figure 9.1). These sites have many features of a standalone website (pages, images, links, widgets) but don't require that you set up a web server or pay for a host. If you are interested in creating a site that needs to be as inexpensive as possible and won't get much traffic, this is definitely an option. It won't have all the bells and whistles, but it will do exactly what you need.

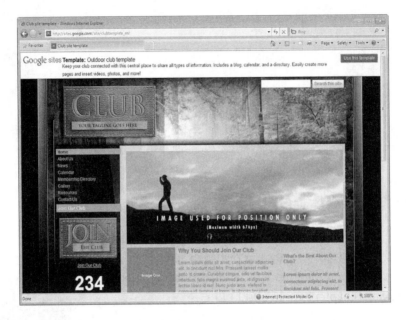

FIGURE 9.1
The outdoor club template from Google.

This chapter covers how to sign up for and build sites that use these web page services, and it discusses the features and limitations of each of these sites. They are all free, but each has different features, so explore them all before making a choice.

> **note** These web page services are always being updated and improved, so the instructions and images in this book might appear slightly different from what's on your computer screen.

Google Sites

We all know that Google.com is pretty much the standard in web search engines, but did you know it also has a web page service? The web page service is called Google Sites, and it was released in 2008. Google Sites is actually based on the web page service of a company Google purchased called Jotspot. This section covers how to sign up for Google Sites, define a website address, create pages, and apply themes.

Signing Up for Google Sites

Google Sites uses an existing Google account or allows you to create a new one.

If you already have a Google account (for Gmail, Google Reader, or Google Groups), all you need to do is use the same email and password for Google Sites. If you have a Google account, skip this section and move on to "Creating a Google Site," which appears later in this chapter.

> **tip** If you are doing any work on the web these days, it is essential to have a Google account. It allows you access to all of Google's sites, and it's free!

To sign up for a new Google account, start at the Google Sites home page.

1. Open a browser and type http://sites.google.com/. This opens the Google Sites home page (see Figure 9.2).

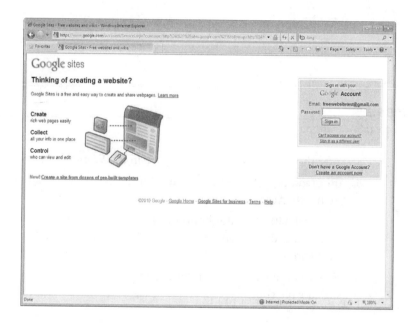

FIGURE 9.2

The Google Sites home page.

2. Click the Sign Up For Sites link. This takes you to the Create an Account page (see Figure 9.3).

3. In the Required Information for Google Account section, enter a current email address and a password, and then re-enter the password.

4. In the next section, Get Started with Google Sites, you have the option of entering your location. There's also a word verification, and you can read the Google Sites Terms of Service.

FIGURE 9.3

The Create an Account page.

5. Enter the word you see in the picture in the Word Verification field.

6. After reading yet another thrilling Terms of Service, click the I Accept. Create My Account button.

7. An email with the information verifying your account is sent to the email account you provided. Read this email and follow the instructions.

8. After you have logged in, return to the Google Sites home page (sites.google.com).

Creating a Google Site

After you have logged in to your Google account, return to the Google Sites home page so you can begin building your first Google Site.

1. Open your browser to http://sites.google.com/ and click the Create a Site from Dozens of Pre-Built Templates button. This opens the Create New Site page (see Figure 9.4). This page takes you through the beginning steps of setting up a Google Site.

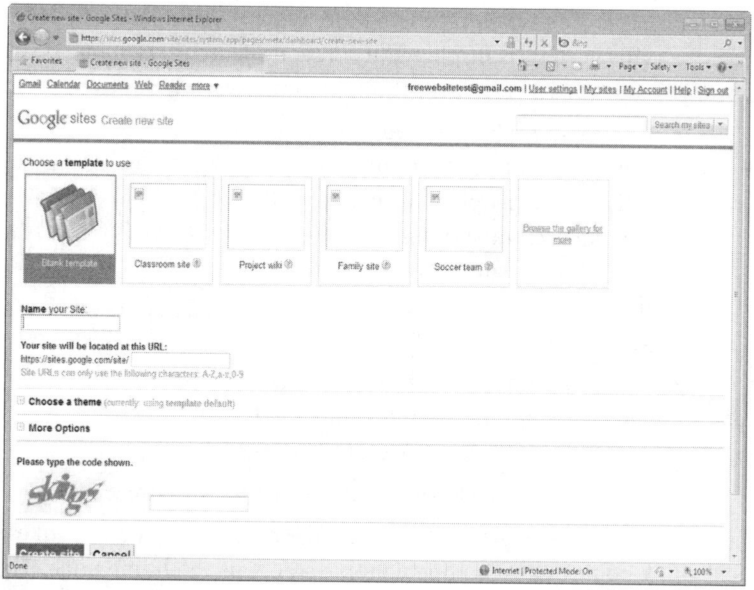

FIGURE 9.4
The Create New Site page.

2. The first thing Google Sites asks you to do is select a template. A template makes your job a lot easier, so take the time to look at them before choosing.

3. In the Site Name field, enter the name of your Google Site. This can be anything you want it to be, but make sure it is a good representation of your content.

4. Define your site uniform resource locator (URL). This is how people will find your site. Google Sites creates a URL based on your site title as a suggestion, but you can change this. The URL can include numbers or letters (both lowercase and uppercase), but it can't have spaces. This comes at the end of http://sites.google.com/site/.

> **note** You can't have your own domain name with Google Sites. Your site has to exist under the umbrella of Google Sites. If you want your own domain name, this and other web page services might not be for you.

5. Google Sites has preloaded Site Themes. These themes give your website color and personality. There are about two dozen themes at the moment, but Google adds more all the time.

6. Click the plus sign beside More Options, and enter a site description. This is what is displayed if someone searches for your site. It also helps you have a clear definition, in your own mind, of your website.

7. Choose to make your website either private or public. A private site allows only people you specify (with Google accounts) access to your site. Having your site open to the public means anyone can see it and search for it.

> **note** By default, Google Sites sets up two pages for you. The first page is the home page; the second is a site map that automatically creates a list of the pages on your website and the way they are connected.

8. If your site includes or may include mature content (adult graphics, text, or sounds), check the Mature Content box.

9. Enter the text code shown to verify that you are a real person.

10. Click Create Site. This creates the basics for your site, takes you to the Google Site web page editor, and opens the home page. The Google Sites page viewer (see Figure 9.5) is what you use to create your site.

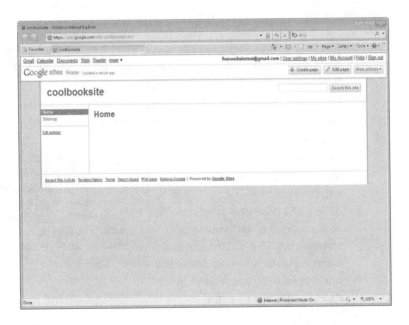

FIGURE 9.5

The Google Sites page viewer.

Editing a Page

You can edit each page in your Google Site separately. You can add a number of elements, enter and format text, add a table, or change the page layout. Just follow these steps:

1. Open sites.google.com and select your site under the list of My Sites.

2. Select Home from the navigation list.

3. Click the Edit Page button. This opens the Edit Page editing tool (see Figure 9.6). Use this tool to edit the text on the page, including the title and body text.

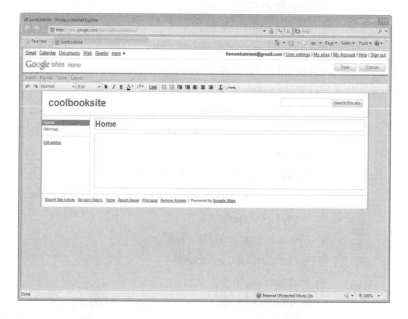

FIGURE 9.6

The Google Sites page editor.

4. If you want to change the web page title, click the title area and edit the text.

5. To add or edit text to the body of a web page, click in the body area and enter the text. You can use the text formatting toolbar to set the font type, size, bold, italic, underline, color, or highlight. You can also use this toolbar to view and edit the page's Hypertext Markup Language (HTML).

6. If you want to add some special features to the web page, use the Insert drop-down menu. Each of the available objects is useful in different situations, so have fun with them. You can add the following to a website:

- Image
- Link
- Table of contents
- Subpage listing
- Horizontal line
- Google AdSense object
- Google Calendar object
- Google Document object
- Google Map object
- Picasa photo
- Picasa web slideshow
- Google Presentation object
- Google Spreadsheet object
- Google Spreadsheet Form object
- Google Video object (Google video or YouTube video)
- Recent Post gadget
- Recently Updated Files gadget
- Recent List Items gadget
- Text Box gadget
- More (click to see the latest Google gadgets)

7. If you want to format text in ways not available on the text formatting bar, select the text and then use the Format drop-down.

8. If you want to insert a table or edit an existing one, use the Table drop-down.

9. If you want to change the layout of the page, you can use the Layout drop-down to choose a one- or two-column layout.

10. When you're finished, click the Save button. Your page is now displayed with your changes.

Creating a Page

Your Google Site starts with your home page, but you are free to add more pages. To add a new page, follow these steps:

1. Click the CreatePage button to add a new web page to your Google Site. This opens the Create a New Page screen (see Figure 9.7).

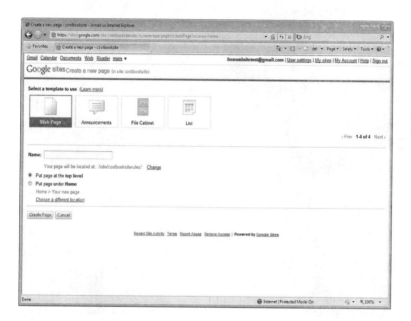

FIGURE 9.7

The Create a New Page screen.

2. Select the type of page you wish to add: Web Page, Announcements, File Cabinet, or List.

3. In the Name field, enter the page's title.

4. If you want the page to be at the same level as your home page, select Put Page at the Top Level. If you want the new web page under your home page, select the second option.

5. Click Create Page. This adds the page and opens it in Edit mode.

Move a Page

As you are creating more pages, you may need to move the pages around. To move a page, do the following:

1. From the More Actions menu, click Move. The Move Page screen opens (see Figure 9.8). You use this screen to drag the page where you want it.

2. Click Move.

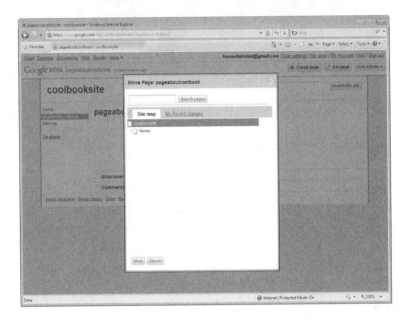

FIGURE 9.8
The Move Page screen.

Delete a Page

You might create a page that you later don't need. To delete a page, do this:

1. From the More Actions menu, click Delete. Google Sites makes sure you want to delete the page.

2. Click Delete Page. The page is deleted.

Edit Page Settings

Each page has its own settings. These include showing the page in navigation bars, showing the page title and links to other pages, and allowing comments.

You can also change the page URL. To edit page settings, follow these steps:

1. From the More Actions menu, click Page Settings. The Page Settings screen opens (see Figure 9.9).

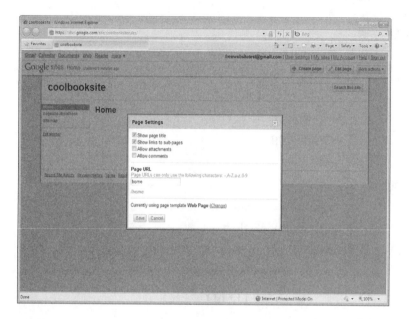

FIGURE 9.9

The Page Settings screen.

2. Edit the settings you want.

3. Click Save.

Edit Site Settings

As with each page, there are a number of Google Site settings you can change. These include the following:

- Site sharing
- Appearance
- Other settings, such as the options you set when you set up the site

You can access all these settings through the More Actions button by selecting Manage Site.

Google Sites Features and Limitations

You need to be aware of some features and limitations with Google Sites before making your decision to stick with it.

Features

- Single-click page creation
- No HTML required
- 10 Gigabytes of storage
- Themes
- Page sharing

Limitations

- Cannot use a domain name
- Must use Google themes
- Has a limited structure
- Cannot copy parts of the site

Wetpaint

If you are looking to set up a simple social network or wiki, you may want to look at Wetpaint. This service, started in 2005, is specifically designed to create fan sites for various bands, TV shows, movies, or celebrities. This section covers how to sign up for the service and edit pages.

Signing Up for Wetpaint

To use Wetpaint, you need to sign up for a Wetpaint account. Start at the Wetpaint home page:

1. Open a browser and type http://www.wetpaint.com/. This opens the Wetpaint home page (see Figure 9.10).
2. Click the Go button at the top of the page. This takes you to the Sign Up page (see Figure 9.11).

FIGURE 9.10

The Wetpaint home page.

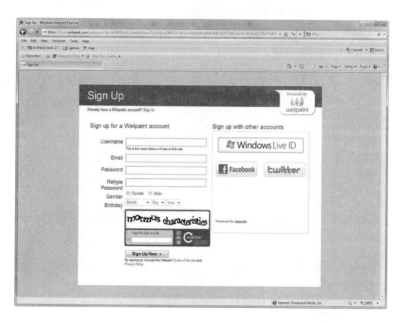

FIGURE 9.11

The Sign Up page.

3. Enter your username, email, password (twice), gender, date of birth, and code displayed on the page.

4. Click the Sign Up Now button.

Creating a Site on Wetpaint

After you have created your Wetpaint account, you can begin building your first Wetpaint site (see Figure 9.12):

1. Enter your site name, URL, description and category.

2. Choose who can see your site. This can be anyone, people who join your site specifically, or only site creators.

3. Click the Continue to Step 2: The Fun Part button.

4. Select a style for your website and click the Continue to Step 3 button.

5. Finally, enter the words that appear in the graphic to prove you are a human.

6. Once the site is created, click on the Go to My Site button.

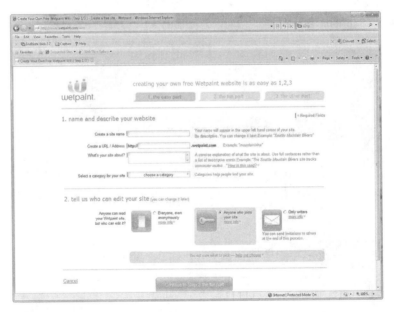

FIGURE 9.12

The site creation page.

Editing a Page

You can edit each page in your Wetpaint site separately. You can add a number of elements, enter and format text, or change the page layout. To edit your pages, follow these steps:

1. Open www.wetpaint.com and click My Wetpaint Sites at the top of the page. Select the site you want to edit.

2. Click the Easy Edit button. This opens the page editing tool (see Figure 9.13). This looks like your page, but all the text is editable. Use this tool to edit the text on the page, including the title and body text.

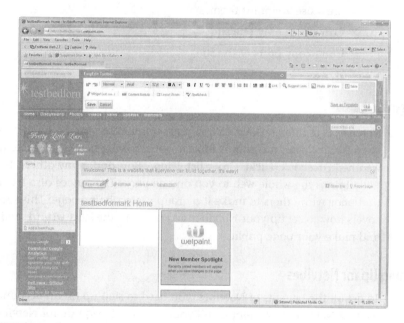

FIGURE 9.13

The Wetpaint page editor.

3. When finished, click the Save button. Your page is now displayed with your changes.

Wetpaint Features and Limitations

You should be aware of some Wetpaint features and limitations before making a decision to stick with it.

Features

- Simple and elegant interface
- Themes
- Photos

Limitations

- No HTML allowed
- Can't use a domain name
- Must use Wetpaint themes
- Can create only one site
- Can't copy parts of the site

Netvibes

Netvibes is a different kind of web page creation service. It enables you to create a start page that contains links to your favorite news sources, to-do list, weather, Facebook, Flickr, Craigslist, Digg, eBay, and many others. It essentially brings the whole web to you on one page. The service also lets you share that page with others to make it a group project home page. This section covers how to set up your Netvibes account, run the start wizard, add content, and make your page public.

Signing Up for Netvibes

To get all the benefits of Netvibes, you need to sign up for an account. This enables Netvibes to remember all your settings. To sign up for Netvibes, follow these instructions:

1. Open a browser and go to www.netvibes.com/. This opens the default Netvibes start page (see Figure 9.14). Netvibes has some excellent default features (such as news, weather, and stock market information).

2. Click Sign In at the top-right corner. This opens the login window.

3. To create a new account, click Sign Up. This opens the Sign Up window (see Figure 9.15).

4. Enter your email and password, and then confirm the password.

5. After reading them (or not), agree with the Terms of Service.

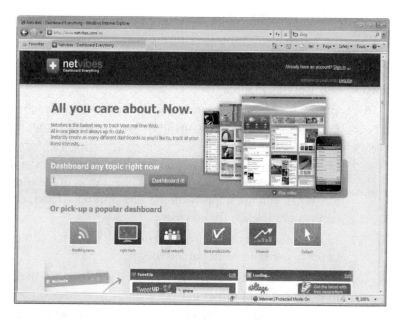

FIGURE 9.14

The Netvibes start page.

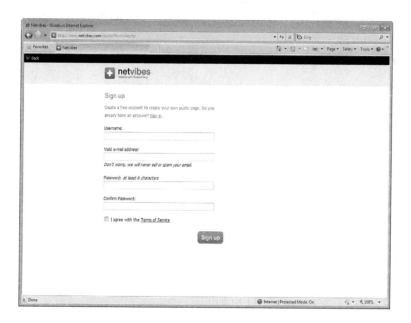

FIGURE 9.15

The Netvibes Sign Up page.

6. Click Sign Up. An email is sent to you to confirm your email address. Follow the instructions to complete the setup of your Netvibes account.

Personalizing Your Netvibes Page

After confirming your email address, you are taken to the Netvibes home page. The page already has some useful widgets loaded for you. Follow these steps to personalize your page:

1. Click Edit next to General on the tab in the upper-left part of the screen. This allows you to choose the orientation of the widgets you use. When you are happy with the way your page looks, click the red X on the right to close the edit view.

2. You can now edit any individual widget by using the Edit link located in the upper-right corner of the widget.

3. You can delete any widgets you do not like by clicking the (X) button in the upper-right corner of the widget.

4. To add new widgets, click on the green Add Content button in the upper left of the screen. Then choose the option you want, and click the (Add) button underneath. When you are finished adding widgets, click the red (X) button in the right corner.

HTML 101

HTML is the common language of the web. It is the programming language of every web page on the Internet. To do anything on the web, you need a solid grounding in how HTML works and how others use it.

HTML stands for Hypertext Markup Language. "Hypertext" means there are links between documents and within documents that interconnect the documents. Linked pages allow the web to constantly expand and become more interconnected. A markup language uses tags to "mark up" the text to apply formatting and structure. A tag is essentially a text marker that signifies the start and the end of a particular kind of formatting.

HTML was created in 1991 by Tim Berners-Lee, a researcher at a scientific think tank called CERN, located in Switzerland. Tim wanted to create a simple system of document organization that allowed for simplicity and cross referencing. When other people began using HTML, it took off, and the web as we know it was born.

If you've never done any type of programming, you're probably thinking it's much too difficult to pick up in one chapter (see Figure 10.1). On the contrary, HTML is easy if you understand the basics and keep things simple. My background is not in math or engineering. Like millions of other people, I learned HTML by reading about it and experimenting. HTML is a great sandbox in which to learn things.

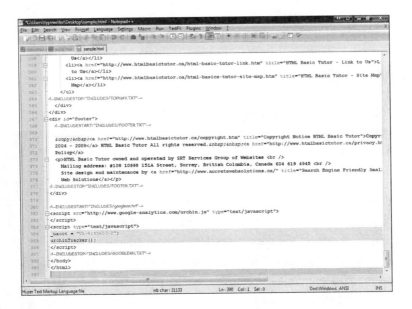

FIGURE 10.1
A complex HTML page.

This chapter covers the basics of how HTML works, common HTML tags, and HTML editors. All these things can help you create web pages and understand what other people have created.

HTML is also in a constant state of change. For this reason, I have added information about the latest version of HTML and what it means to a beginning web developer.

The Structure of HTML

Your first look at the underlying code of a web page can be baffling. Why? Because without an understanding of how HTML works, it's difficult to interpret what's going on. So the first step in figuring all this out is learning the basic parts of HTML.

As mentioned previously, HTML is a markup language. You use tags to "mark up" text. A browser then interprets these tags, and the correct formatting and structures are displayed on the web page. The web browser doesn't display the code, but rather the coded content, based on the HTML you created.

The Structure of Tags

A tag is a text label applied to a block of text. A tag has three parts:

- **The opening tag**—The beginning of a tag is signified with a < sign. This is then followed by the tag name and a >. For example, `<bold>`.

- **The text affected by the tag**—Anything contained within the tag has the formatting or structure applied to it.

- **The closing tag**—This ends the tag affecting the text. It is made up of a < and then a / to signify closure, the tag name, and then a >. For example, `</bold>`.

For example, take this block of text:

The quick brown fox jumped over the lazy dog.

This is just plain text. Add the tags and it looks like this:

The <bold>quick</bold> brown fox jumped over the lazy dog.

> **tip** Notice how the tags add no spaces to the displayed text. It is as if they are not there. Keep this in mind when creating your HTML.

Viewed in the browser, the text becomes

The **quick** brown fox jumped over the lazy dog.

Tags can be nested within each other. For example,

The <italics><bold>quick</bold> brown fox</italics> jumped over the lazy dog.

produces text that looks like this:

The ***quick brown fox*** jumped over the lazy dog.

The `</italics>` tag is applied to all the text within the tag, including the bold text.

This is the same for any tag or set of tags. What is between the tag has the formatting for the tag applied to it.

The next section covers the most commonly used tags—what they do and how to use them.

Common HTML Tags

It is important to familiarize yourself with a few commonly used HTML tags. The following list contains these commonly used HTML tags, organized into categories. Each tag is accompanied by a description, an example of the code, and an example of the result where appropriate.

HTML Structure Tags

The following sections describe the tags that make up the structure and frame of your web page.

HTML `<html></html>`

All other HTML tags must be contained in this tag. This should be the first and last tag in your document.

Header `<head></head>`

This tag defines the structure of the header of the HTML document. It never appears in the browser but contains title information, scripting, and other formatting information.

Title `<title></title>`

This is the web page title. This text appears on the title bar of your browser. It should appear within the Header tag.

Body `<body></body>`

This is the entire body of your web page. Anything you want to show up on the page must be contained in a Body tag.

Comment `<!-- -->`

This tag enables you to document your code. Documenting means adding notes in your code that explain what different parts of the code do. Developers use this to communicate with the people reading their code or as notes for their own reference. This makes it easy to make sense of large HTML documents. Document your code as much as possible. Comments are never displayed on your web page but help in the editing process. For example,

```
<!-- This is the body section of my web page -->
```

Division `<div></div>`

This tag assigns divisions to the body of the web page. You can then apply formatting to these divisions. The `<div>` tag does not show up in the browser, but the effects of it do. Use it to apply formatting to different divisions of your web page. For more information on the `<div>` tag, consult Chapter 13, "Building a Site Using HTML."

Text Tags

These tags affect the text in the body of your page.

Font `<font></font>`

This tag defines the size, color, and typeface contained in the tag. Each of these specific details is defined within the start tag. For example, if you want Arial text, size 8, and red, the tag would be

```
<font face="arial" color="red" size="8"></font>
```

caution Don't use any old font face you have on your computer in this tag. It might work correctly on your machine, but you don't know what your visitors have on their machines. If the font is not on the visitor's machine, the browser displays the default font of the browser, and the page might not display as you intended.

Bold `<bold></bold>`

This tag bolds text. It makes text appear darker and slightly larger than regular text.

For example, `The <bold>quick</bold> brown fox.` produces

The **quick** brown fox.

Italics `<italic></italic>`

This tag italicizes text. It makes text appear slanted to the right.

For example, `The <italic>quick</italic> brown fox.` produces

The *quick* brown fox.

Strikethrough `<strike></strike>`

This tag creates strikethrough text, which means there is a line running through the text.

For example, `The <strike>quick</strike> brown fox.` produces

The ~~quick~~ brown fox.

Underline `<u></u>`

This tag underlines text. A line appears under all the text.

For example, `The <u>quick</u> brown fox.` produces

The <u>quick</u> brown fox.

Subscript `<sub></sub>`

This tag creates text that appears below the line of other text.

For example, `The <sub>quick</sub> brown fox.` produces

The $_{quick}$ brown fox.

Superscript `<sup></sup>`

This tag results in text appearing above the line of other text.

For example, `The <sup>quick</sup> brown fox.` produces

The ^{quick} brown fox.

Center `<center></center>`

This tag centers text.

For example, `<center>The quick brown fox. </center>` produces

The quick brown fox.

Heading `<h#></h#>` (# Is a Number from 1–6)

This formats the text contained within the tag into one of six headings. These headings organize your text in the same way you would see in a typical document. The headings correspond to hierarchical levels; therefore, H1 is larger and more prominent than H2, which is more prominent than H3, and so on.

For example, `<h1>The</h1><h2>quick</h2>brown<h3>fox.</h3>` produces

The

quick

brown

fox.

Paragraph <p></p>

This tag defines a paragraph and includes formatting and spacing of the paragraph.

For example, `<p>The quick brown fox jumps over the lazy dog.</p>` produces

The quick brown fox jumps over the lazy dog.

Horizontal Rule <hr>

A horizontal rule runs across the page.

For example, `The quick brown fox. <hr>` produces

The quick brown fox.

Line Break

This tag breaks a line of text. You might want to use this to have text line up and break the way you want it to instead of letting the browser break it up by default.

For example, `The quick <br>brown fox.` produces

The quick

brown fox.

Nonbreaking Space

This tag inserts a space in text where you need it. For example, `The quick` adds a space between the words *the* and *quick*.

Lists

Lists in HTML come in two flavors: unordered (that is, with bullets) or ordered (that is, with numbers). The first thing you need to do is define text as a list and then define the elements of that list. Each of these things has its own tag that works with the other tags to create the list. First, I will cover the tags and then show how to put them together.

Order List <ol></ol>

This creates a list that has numbers for each list item.

Unorder List `<ul></ul>`

This creates a list that has bullets for each list item.

List Item `<li></li>`

This defines a list item.

So, here's what the HTML code for a list looks like:

```
<ol>
<li>Item </li>
<li>Item </li>
<li>Item </li>
</ol>
<ul>
<li>Item </li>
<li>Item </li>
<li>Item </li>
</ul>
```

And here is how the list is displayed on the web page:

1. Item
2. Item
3. Item

- Item
- Item
- Item

Tables

Tables are like lists. They combine several tags to make one table, just as several tags make one list. Tables are made up of rows and columns. The table can also have a header row that acts like a title row. Again, I will describe the table tags and then put them together in code.

Table `<table></table>`

This tag surrounds the table and defines its limits. Properties of the table are also defined within this tag—things like border, alignment, and width.

Table Row <tr></tr>

This defines one row of the table.

Table Cell <td></td>

This defines each cell in a table row.

Table Header <th></th>

This defines a row as a header and is displayed in bold type.

So, to create a table that has three rows and two columns, the HTML code would look like this:

```
<table border="1">
    <tr>
        <th>Cell 1</th>
        <th>Cell 2</th>
    </tr>
    <tr>
        <td>Cell 3</td>
        <td>Cell 4</td>
    </tr>
    <tr>
        <td>Cell 5</td>
        <td>Cell 6</td>
    </tr>
</table>
```

This creates a table that displays like this:

Cell 1	Cell 2
Cell 3	Cell 4
Cell 5	Cell 6

Geek Speak

nest

A nested table means a table is contained within the cell of another table. This allows you to make complex structures needed for page formatting.

Tables can get much more complicated than this. You can *nest* tables within tables to create complex structures for displaying information.

Hyperlinks

Hyperlinks are defined as anchors and references in HTML. An anchor is the hyperlinked text or graphic, and a reference is where you are taken when you click on the hyperlink. Text and graphics can serve as anchors. References can be within an HTML document or to another document.

A hyperlink is made up of these parts: an anchor tag, a reference, and the text or image that is hyperlinked. For instance:

```
Follow this <a href="http://www.flickr.com">link</a>
```

This creates a hyperlink for the word *link* that goes to http://www.flickr.com. To open the link in a new window, add a target in the anchor tag:

```
Follow this <a href="http://www.flickr.com" target="_blank">link</a>
```

The link now opens a new window.

In the browser, the hyperlinked text appears blue and underlined by default. If it is an image, it is outlined in blue. When you put your mouse over a hyperlink, it turns from an arrow to a small hand.

Images

Images do not appear in HTML code. What appears are references to files. These references might be on the local web server or elsewhere on the web. For example:

```
<img src="angry.gif" />
```

This displays the image file `angry.gif` if the file is in the same directory as the HTML file.

Free HTML Editors

Now that you understand the basics of HTML, you'll want to begin creating and editing HTML code. You can use a number of free HTML editors, and they fall into two categories: text editors and WYSIWYG (what you see is what you get) editors. A text editor edits HTML code directly; a WYSIWYG editor builds HTML code for you.

Text Editors

Text editors enable you to work directly in the HTML code. This makes it easy for you to search the text document, find exactly what you're looking for, and quickly make your edits. With a WYSIWYG editor, the code you want to change can be hard to find. I prefer to edit HTML code using a text editor. Here are some common text editors:

- **Notepad (Windows)**—This comes standard with the Windows operating system.

- **Notepad ++ (Windows, Linux)**—http://notepad-plus.sourceforge.net/uk/site.htm. The best text editor around.

- **TextWrangler (Mac)**—www.barebones.com/products/textwrangler/index.shtml (see Figure 10.2). A nice Mac text editor.

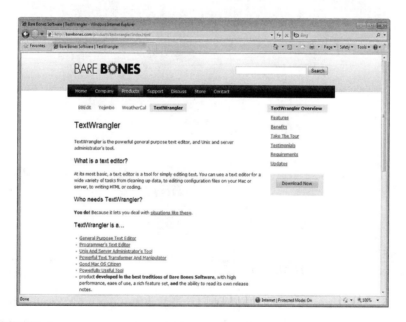

FIGURE 10.2

An excellent Mac text editor.

- **XEmacs (Windows, Linux, UNIX)**—www.xemacs.org/index.html. Another great text editor.

WYSIWYG Editors

These editors build web pages graphically and build the code for you. You build the web page as it will be seen in the browser, and WYSIWYG browsers create the code for you. These editors make doing things such as creating complex tables incredibly simple. Unfortunately, they can also fill your HTML with needless tags, but they are ideal for beginners. Here are a few major ones:

- KompoZer (Windows, Mac, Linux)—www.kompozer.net (see Figure 10.3)

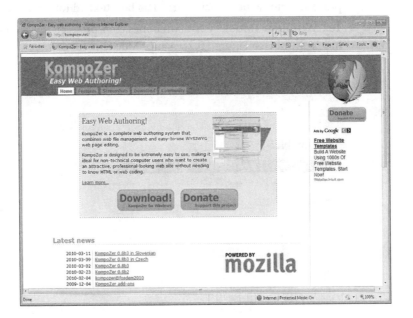

FIGURE 10.3
An open-source graphic HTML editor.

- Quanta Plus (Windows, Linux)—http://quanta.kdewebdev.org
- Bluefish (Windows, Mac, Linux)—http://bluefish.openoffice.nl
- OpenLaszlo (Windows, Mac, Linux)—www.openlaszlo.org

Resources

This chapter just scratches the surface of HTML. There is so much more to learn, and the more you learn, the more you can do with your websites.

Here are some resources to further your understanding of HTML:

- **W3Schools (www.w3schools.com)**—Probably the best, most concise HTML teaching tool on the Internet (see Figure 10.4). Bookmark this site because you will return to it often.

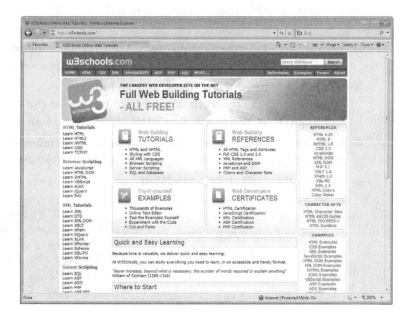

FIGURE 10.4
W3Schools is one of the best HTML resources on the Internet.

- **Webmonkey HTML Cheat Sheet (www.webmonkey.com/2010/02/html_cheatsheet)**—This is another excellent source for beginners.
- **If you know nothing about HTML, this is where you start (www.htmlgoodies.com/primers/html/article.php/3478131)**—The title says it all. This is an excellent collection of HTML primers.
- **HTML Basic Tutor (www.htmlbasictutor.ca)**—This site is like having your very own HTML tutor.

The Latest Version of HTML

Just like software programs, HTML has different versions, the latest of which is in development as HTML5. With each version, new features, tags, and browser compatibility issues are introduced. HTML5 is still in development, but even the newest web developer should be aware of what is going on. The goal of HTML5 is to better integrate multimedia into websites. Before adding HTML5 content to your website, make sure you test it on as many browsers as possible. To help you, I have added some of the new tags to Appendix A, "List of the Most Common HTML Tags." I have also added some HTML5 references here.

- **WC3 HTML5 Reference (http://dev.w3.org/html5/html-author)**—This is the most complete and most up-to-date information on HTML5.

- **HTML5 Unleashed: Tips, Tricks, and Techniques (www.w3avenue.com/2010/05/07/html5-unleashed-tips-tricks-and-techniques)**—A nice overview of HTML5 features in plain language.

- **HTML5 Quick Reference Guide (http://veign.com/reference/html5-guide.php)**—A quick reference guide for HTML5 developers.

- **THE HTML5 TEST (http://html5test.com/)**—Use this site to test the HTML5 capabilities of your browser. It breaks down all the new HTML5 features and tells you if your browser can use them.

note HTML5 is brand new software that can change at any second. Be careful using any of its code.

Working with Images

Believe it or not, prior to 1993, the Internet was mainly text based. For some of you, this might seem almost unbelievable. Since then, the Internet has become a very visual place, full of color and vivid imagery.

This chapter covers the different types of images, what programs you can use with them, how to use them on web pages, and where to find them.

You should understand some terms before we start:

■ **Pixels**—Like atoms that make up matter, pixels make up digital images. A pixel is the smallest piece of information in a digital image and is one color. Every image can be described as a certain number of pixels high and a certain number wide (see Figure 11.1).

FIGURE 11.1
This image is 150 pixels high and 300 pixels wide.

- **Resolution**—An image's resolution is the number of pixels that make up a square inch. The higher the resolution, the larger the file size. The most common resolution is 72 pixels per inch.

- **RGB**—Red, green, blue. This is a mode of creating colors by mixing red, green, and blue in certain amounts. Each of the three colors has values from 0 to 255. Using this method, more than 16 million colors are available to you. For more information on color, refer to Chapter 4, "Designing Your Site."

- **Hexadecimal**—A method of taking three-digit RGB numbers and converting them to two-digit numbers that HTML can understand.

Web Graphics

There are almost as many image file types used on the web as there are web pages. This section covers the top three file formats. Unless you are doing something completely out of the ordinary, you should keep to these formats.

Lossy and Lossless Compression

I recommend that you always try to keep the size of the file small. An HTML file with 100 words can be as little as 8,192 bytes, whereas a small image file that is 100 pixels by 100 pixels (roughly the size of a postage stamp) can be almost half that many bytes. Image compression tries to make your files as small as possible while retaining quality. Lossy compression degrades the image slightly to make the size of the file smaller. Lossless compression has no degradation, so usually the file sizes are not as reduced as in lossy compression. Here is a list of the most common file types:

- **Graphics Interchange Format (.gif)**—This is a lossless file format that is common on the web. These files can be saved with a maximum of only 256 colors, making it a better file format for graphics rather than photographs (see Figure 11.2). You can make one color on a .gif transparent (the background shows through), and you can animate .gif files. Animated .gifs are covered later in this chapter.

- **Portable Network Graphics (.png)**—This lossless image format is replacing .gif and becoming more common on the web. Like a .gif, a .png can be transparent. It can be larger than a .gif or a .jpg.

FIGURE 11.2

An example of a graphic that might be best saved as a .gif.

■ **Joint Photographic Experts Group (.jpg or .jpeg)**—This is a lossy file format, but that doesn't mean it is bad. It just uses math to determine patterns so that you can reduce the image size. More compression, though, means lower image quality. A .jpg can display millions of colors at once. This format is mainly used for photographs. It is the most common file format used on the web. A picture I took in San Antonio, shown in Figure 11.3, is an example of a graphic saved as a .jpg.

FIGURE 11.3

An example of a graphic that might be best saved as a .jpg.

The Image Tag

To add images to a web page, use the HTML tag IMG. This tag has several properties, or attributes. Attributes are the things that define how the image is displayed. The following table lists some of the more common attributes.

Attribute	Description	Notes	Example
src	A mandatory attribute that is the file location and full name of the image you want displayed.	This needs to be the exact location of the file in relation to the HTML file on the server.	`<img src="logo.gif" />`
alt	Alternative text to display if the image is not being displayed.		`<img src="logo.gif" alt="Logo" />`
align	Specifies how the image is placed in relation to text. The values can be top, bottom, middle, left, and right.	Wraps the text around images.	`<img src="logo.gif" align="top" />`
border	The pixel width of the border around the image.	The border is always black.	`<img src="logo.gif" border="3" />`
height	Changes the height of the image to this number of pixels or percentage of original image.	This stretches or shrinks the image to this pixel size without scaling the width, so the image may distort. Do not use if possible.	`<img src="logo.gif" height="300" />`
width	Changes the width of the image to this many pixels or percentage of original image.	This stretches or shrinks the image to this pixel size without scaling the height, so the image may distort. Do not use if possible.	`<img src="logo.gif" width="300" />`
ismap	Designates the image as a server-side image map.	For more on image maps, see the "Image Maps" section in this chapter.	
usermap	Designates the image as a client-side image map.	For more on image maps, see the "Image Maps" section in this chapter.	
longdesc	A link to a URL containing the long description of the image.	Rarely used.	`<img src="logo.gif" longdesc="longdesc.htm" />`
hspace	Defines the horizontal space around the image in pixels.	This adds a margin of space on the sides of an image.	`<img src="logo.gif" hspace="2" />`
vspace	Defines the vertical space around the image in pixels.	This adds a margin of space on the top and bottom of an image.	`<img src="logo.gif" vspace="2" />`

11

Look at the images on different websites (by viewing the source of the website) and see how they use the image tag. As an example, this image tag came off a news site:

```
<img hspace="0" height="239" border="0" width="265" vspace="0" alt="A "
➥src="images/candidate.jpg"/>
```

Background Images

You can use an image as the background of an entire page. Background images use the BODY tag and the background attribute. Although that was all the rage when the attribute was introduced, it is now considered old fashioned or tacky. If you're going to use a background image, use a CSS. For more on using a cascading style sheet (CSS), see Chapter 13, "Building a Site Using HTML."

Image Maps

An image map is an HTML structure that allows you to specify coordinates on an image connected to hyperlinks. An image map can be server side (that is, there are files stored on the server that assist with the image map) or client side (all the information for the image map is stored in the HTML file).

The client-side image map uses the MAP and AREA tags within the HTML code to define the actions taken when clicking on a certain area of the image.

You can even find sites online to help build your image map. The Online Image Map Generator (www.maschek.hu/imagemap/imgmap), shown in Figure 11.4, enables you to define client-side image maps easily and generates the code for you.

Animated GIFs

Animated gifs are a series of .gif files saved into one larger .gif file that animate when loaded into a web browser. Use these sparingly, if at all, because they can be large files that slow down the load time of your page and are perceived as tacky attention-getters. If you need to add an animated .gif, use a free online animated .gif creator like gickr (http://gickr.com/).

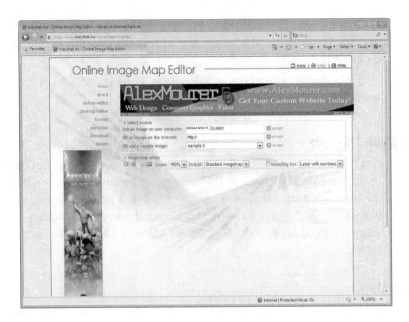

FIGURE 11.4
The Online Image Map Editor.

Optimizing Images

As I said earlier, your site should have the best images with the lowest file sizes. In the end, it is a trade-off. Sometimes that high-resolution photograph with millions of colors makes your site come together and look spectacular, but other times it is important to have the fastest-loading site possible.

Resizing Images

Do not resize your images in HTML. The height and width tags mentioned earlier should never be used. If you use these attributes to change the size of an image, the entire original image is loaded, then resized, so there is no benefit from using those attributes.

When to Use Different File Types

As mentioned earlier, whenever possible, use the highest level of compression and lowest number of colors you can. Photos should be .jpg and graphics should be .gifs.

Slicing Images

Larger images can be sliced into smaller images so they load more quickly. This is certainly effective when parts of a large area are not central to your design. When you do slice images, make sure your image lines up when it is completely loaded.

Finding Images

You might feel like a kid in a candy store when looking for images on the web. It's certainly easy to find images, but it is not legal or moral to use them without the permission of the person to whom they belong. People add images to the web constantly and don't realize that there are people out there who take them without asking. Let me be clear: It's illegal to use images for which you have not obtained permission.

Free Images

There are sites that offer free images. This is good because you can use the images free of charge and with the owner's permission. The problem is they are usually not the best images and may appear on other websites. If you plan on using free images, you have to do quite a bit of looking to find just what you want, but you can't beat the price.

When using images from these sites, remember to read all the rules and fine print to protect yourself. Here are some of the better free image sites:

- **Creative Commons (http://search.creativecommons.org)**—Creative Commons is a group dedicated to changing copyright and ownership. This site lets you search Creative Commons licensed content.
- **Kave Wall (www.kavewall.com)**—A great site for free backgrounds and textures.
- **freestockphotography (www.adigitaldreamer.com/gallery/index.php)**—Images that are free and royalty free.
- **visipix.com (http://visipix.dynalias.com/index_hidden.htm)**—High-resolution images with free copyright for private and commercial use.

Other People's Images

If you find an image on the web that you want to use, contact the person who owns the image and explain who you are, what image you want to use, what your website is all about, and why you want to use that image. If you are granted permission, make sure to credit the image owner. If you do not get permission or get no response, don't just go ahead and use the image.

Using Your Own Images

One solution to finding images for your website is to take your own pictures or make your own graphics. This certainly makes it easier for you to credit the creator of the images, but as I said before, someone might take your images. If your images matter to you, be careful where you put them.

11

Working with Multimedia

As we all know, the web is much more than text and pictures; it's also multimedia. Multimedia is the combination of multiple forms of *digitized* media, including video and audio files. For example, a song from a band's website and the trailer of an independent film (see Figure 12.1) are both forms of multimedia. When used properly, multimedia adds to the user's experience. When not used properly, multimedia can ruin a website. This chapter shows you how to prepare multimedia objects for use in your website.

One important consideration when dealing with multimedia files is file size. Multimedia files are usually quite large, and there is a constant battle between keeping the file size small and maintaining high quality. Even though broadband access is becoming common, there are still numerous people who use slower Internet connections. Do not assume that everyone will have lightning-fast connections to download your large movie files.

FIGURE 12.1

QuickTime.com does an excellent job of using multimedia.

Another consideration is that media files can be specific to operating systems. Having a web page that tries to play a file that doesn't work on most operating systems is just going to annoy some of your visitors. When making choices, make sure you consider different operating systems and choose file types that run on the most operating systems.

Geek Speak

digitized

Any multimedia used on the web needs to be digitized, which means that it needs to be put on a computer in a file format the computer understands.

In addition, not all visitors to your site may have the hardware to use multimedia effectively. They may not have speakers or graphics cards that allow all multimedia to play effectively. Don't leave these folks out in the cold. Make multimedia an enhancement on your website, not a requirement.

Finally, multimedia files can be available for download or streaming. A downloaded multimedia file is transferred to a computer where a media player can play it. Streamed media files are played while downloading, usually through a browser. What you use depends on the size and content of your multimedia files.

This chapter covers the multimedia objects you can use in web pages. This includes how to create, digitize, upload, edit, and use multimedia objects for your website. In Chapter 21, "Building a Multimedia Website," these elements are put together on a website.

Digital Audio Files

When used correctly, audio can enhance the mood of a website. A well-placed bit of audio engages your audience and draws them into the web experience. Bad audio does the opposite or worse. If the audio is too loud or intrusive, it puts visitors off. If the audio is repetitive or not related to the website in a way that makes sense, it annoys your visitors rather than welcomes them.

Some people use audio to add music (like a soundtrack) to their page, but the most common use of audio on the web these days is podcasting. Podcasting is essentially creating audio programs on different topics and distributing them on the web. Chapter 21 covers how to add podcasts to your page.

This section discusses what types of audio files are available, how to play them, and how to digitize them.

Audio Formats

As mentioned previously, audio files come in a number of different types. These file types work with some operating systems but not with others. What you want is the smallest possible file size that works on the largest number of operating systems. As with graphics files, audio files can have different types of compression applied to them. Also, audio files can have different levels of audio quality. For more information on file compression, see Chapter 11, "Working with Images." Here are the most common file types:

- `.wav`—This is the default Windows audio file type. Even though it is the default for Windows, you can use it on most operating systems. It is uncompressed, so it can lead to larger file sizes, but it maintains excellent quality.

- `.mp3`—This is currently the most common file format. It runs on just about any computer that connects to the Internet and is compressed (so it has small file sizes) and produces high-quality output.

- `.wma`—Windows Media Audio. This proprietary Windows format is of high quality and good compression but does not play on all systems.

This is by no means a comprehensive list, but most of the files you encounter and want to use will be in these formats. If you choose another format, be sure to research its benefits and limitations before using it.

You can find a more comprehensive list of audio file formats at www.fileinfo.net/filetypes/audio.

Audio Players

Once you have a format chosen for the audio you are going to use, you need to have a player on your machine. A player is a piece of software on your machine, which may or may not be in your browser, that plays audio files. Most operating systems now have an audio player built into them, but a few open source free audio players have some different features:

- **Songbird (http://getsongbird.com/)**—This high-quality open source audio player uses the same software that runs the Firefox browser (Figure 12.2).

FIGURE 12.2

Songbird is an excellent music player.

- **Winamp (www.winamp.com/)**—This full-featured media player has a robust developer community and tons of features.

Digitizing Audio

To begin the process of using audio for your website, you need to digitize some audio. You can do this in a number of ways:

> **caution** There are obviously copyright laws regarding audio files and who owns them. Here's a simple rule: Do not rip and use music on your website to which you do not own the rights. Unless you are Elton John, don't use his music on your site.

- **Record your own**—By hooking up a microphone or musical instrument to your computer, you can record your own sound files and use them on your website.
- **Rip CDs**—Most audio and media players allow you to "rip" CDs. This means you take the audio from the CD and put it on your computer.
- **Use royalty-free music**—There are different sources for royalty-free audio, both on the web and through CDs. Royalty-free audio is free to use in any way. Search the web for the type of royalty-free audio you want.

Audio Editing

After you have your audio digitized, you'll probably want to trim the beginning or ending, clean up some noise, or add some effects. To do this, you need an audio-editing program. Of course, there are many expensive high-end audio editors out there, but some are free and open source. One such editor is Audacity (http://audacity.sourceforge.net/). It is the most popular open-source audio recorder and editor. It has a lot of features and runs on Windows, Mac, and Linux (Figure 12.3).

After you have your audio file edited, you need to save it in the format that best suits your purposes. For instructions on how to use the audio file on your web page, check out Chapter 21.

12

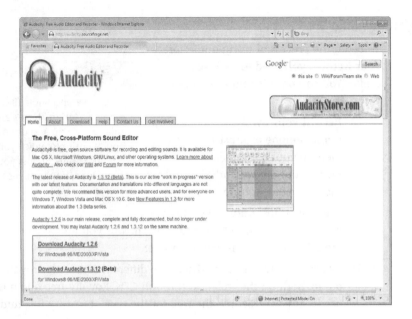

FIGURE 12.3
Audacity is a favorite of multimedia web developers.

Audio Resources

The web is full of incredibly useful audio resources. Audio experts have embraced technology and love to share their knowledge and skills. Here are a few useful links:

- **How to Record Audio for the Web (www.j-learning.org/ present_it/page/how_to_record_audio_for_the_web/_)**—A good overview of how to record audio for the web.

- **Podcast Recording Questions (www.jellycast.com/help-recording. html)**—An excellent introduction to podcasting.

- **Podcasting in Plain English (http://commoncraft.com/ podcasting)**—An excellent video describing the basics of podcasting.

Digital Video Files

Today, everyone seems to be creating video podcasts. They are now ubiquitous on the web. In addition to this, people have started filming themselves, their friends, and their pets—to the amusement of all of us—and posting these videos on the web.

In the past, the process of shooting and editing film was a complicated process. Not anymore. Today people can record high-definition digital video, edit it with professional-quality tools, and post it on YouTube for millions of people to view. Like audio, video has its own unique problems—things like poor quality and long load times. In Chapter 21, I cover how to add video to your page.

This section covers what types of video files are available, how to play them, and how to digitize them.

Video Formats

Like audio, video also comes in many formats, and the format you choose affects the size of the files and the quality of the output. No one wants to watch a tiny video that is fuzzy and skips, nor do they want to wait 15 minutes to watch your homemade video because of the huge file size. It is important to choose the right file type to do this. Here are some of the most common video file types:

- `.avi`—A common video format that can be used with Windows. It can be compressed without a lot of quality loss.
- `.mov`—The QuickTime movie format created by Apple. The standard (and free) QuickTime player is used to play these highly compressed files on either Mac or Windows.
- `.mpeg`—An operating system–independent video format that gives small file sizes and excellent quality.
- `.wmv`—A Windows video format that is becoming more common and has excellent compression.

Remember that you'll want to use a file format that's friendly to most visitors. If you choose another format, be sure to research its benefits and limitations before using it.

For a more comprehensive list of video file formats, go to www.fileinfo.net/filetypes/video.

Video Players

Most operating systems now come with built-in video players. Windows Vista has Media Center and the Mac has iTunes. You also might want to try out a few open-source video players that have different features:

- **VideoLAN (www.videolan.org/)**—A *cross-platform* open-source video player that plays a number of video formats (see Figure 12.4).

12

FIGURE 12.4
Download VideoLAN from here.

■ **Miro (www.getmiro.com/)**—This is an open-source media player that plays video files and has thousands of viewable channels of content, like your TV set.

■ **Kaltura (http://corp.kaltura.com/technology/video_player)**—This is a cool utility that not only plays videos but allows you to annotate them and share those annotations with others.

Geek Speak
cross-platform

Cross-platform means it runs on more than one operating system (operating systems are sometimes called "platforms"). So if a program can run on a Windows machine and a Mac, it is cross-platform.

Digitizing Video

It's easy to digitize video these days. What used to take months and a lot of money now is relatively cheap and takes only a few minutes. The technology behind digitizing video has come a long way. Here are some ways to get digitized video onto your computer:

■ **Use a digital video camera**—Today it is cheap and easy to get a video camera that records directly on digital media such as an *SD card*.

■ **Record on video and import into your computer**—Most video cards today have audio and video inputs to help you digitize video.

■ **Use a webcam**—Today you can buy a camera that plugs directly into your computer and digitize as you record.

■ **Digitize analog video**—Video captured on a video camera and stored on a tape is most likely analog content. To capture this data, use an analog converter such as Dazzle from Pinnacle (www.pinnaclesys. com/PublicSite/us/Products/ Consumer+Products/Dazzle/).

Geek Speak

SD card

An SD card is a small media disk that stores data, including pictures and video. Most computers today come with an SD card reader so you can transfer your data from your camera to another computer.

note Video takes up a huge amount of disk space, so you might want to consider getting an external hard drive to expand your storage capacity.

Video Editing

If you know anything about film or video, you know that using raw video footage is never wise. You need to add titles, rearrange shots, add music, and check audio. There are a number of high-cost video editors out there, but you should never pay for something you can get for free. Here are some free open source video editors:

■ **Cinefx:Jahshaka (http://cinefx.org/)**—This is a cross-platform (Mac, Window, Linux) video editor that offers editing, effects, and audio integration (see Figure 12.5).

■ **Avidemux (www.avidemux.org/)**—This is a simple cross-platform video editing software program. Avidemux has fewer features than Jahshaka but is easier to use.

12

FIGURE 12.5
Editing video with Cinefx:Jahshaka.

If you want to try something new, YouTube now offers a simple video editor (www.youtube.com/editor). This site allows you to combine clips and add audio with a simple drag-and-drop interface. Before doing anything with this page, I would back up all my multimedia files; however, the site is fun and simple to use. Hopefully in the near future, we will see more features from the product.

After you have your video file edited, you need to save it in the format that best suits your purposes.

Video Hosting Sites

When you have your video ready, you can use a video hosting site to share it. These sites have popped up in the past few years and have become some of the most popular sites on the Internet. Here are a couple of the best video sharing sites:

- **YouTube (http://YouTube.com)**—This is the most well-known video hosting site on the web today. It enables you to upload videos, share them with others, and communicate with your viewers.

12

■ **Ustream.tv (www.ustream.tv/)**—A website that lets you share videos or stream live video from your computer (see Figure 12.6).

■ **vimeo (http://vimeo.com/)**—Another video sharing site that lets you connect to your viewers.

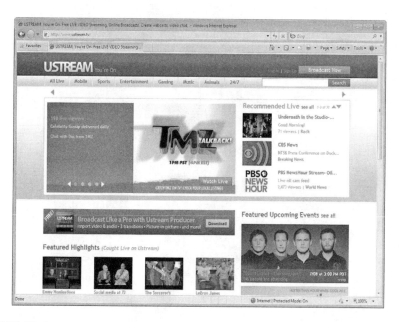

FIGURE 12.6

You can play and stream videos on Ustream.

Video Resources

As I explained, the technology behind video has become much simpler and easier to use and doesn't require as much technical knowledge as it once used to. Nevertheless, there are still some things to learn about it, so I advise you to read up on the subject. The more you know, the better your videos will be. There are numerous websites with bytes and bytes of information on video technology from people with lots of experience. Here are a few to consider:

■ **Video Files & Editing Tutorial**—www.fluffbucket.com/othettutorials/video/format.htm

■ **Web Multimedia Tutorial**—www.w3schools.com/media/default.asp

■ **Web Video Tutorials**—www.webvideozone.com/public/department22.cfm

Building a Site Using HTML

N ow that you have done all your prep work on your web page, you are ready to build a website with Hypertext Markup Language (HTML).

Although it might be rare these days to use only HTML to create a site, it is a good exercise in the fundamentals of website creation. Learning these fundamentals helps you understand how to edit the HTML behind your blog post or family website. Using HTML is still one of the best ways to create a simple web page, and understanding how it works helps you make the edits that produce the results you are looking for.

This chapter covers some of the basics of creating web pages and websites in HTML. You'll see the source code behind a page coded in HTML.

> **note** Before you start to build pages in HTML, you should be familiar with the basics of HTML. This chapter assumes you have read Chapter 10, "HTML 101."

How Web Pages Work

Under every web page on the Internet is at least some HTML. Even a site that uses something like Flash still has an HTML *wrapper* around it.

To really understand the web, you need to understand how web pages work, what parts make up pages, and how these parts work together.

Geek Speak

wrapper

A wrapper is something that surrounds something else. When you buy a chocolate bar, it comes covered in a wrapper. An HTML wrapper works the same way. It surrounds something, such as a Flash object in HTML code, so that a web browser can recognize it.

Page File

Each web page is a file. It might reference other files, but it is still a single file. The web page is just a text file of the HTML commands. This file is small, which is why it loads so quickly.

Extensions

A web page, like most computer files, has an extension. (For more on extensions, see Chapter 5, "Gathering Your Tools"). The extensions for web pages are .htm or .html. Either works fine, but you should choose one for your website and stick with it to make it easy for you to keep your references straight. When you are creating hyperlinks, you need to use the right filename and extension, so staying with one extension makes it easy.

These extensions tell a web browser that the file contains HTML and should be displayed as a web page.

Tools for Creating Web Pages

You can use a couple of different types of tools for HTML creation. These include both text editors and WYSIWYG (what you see is what you get) editors. Most web developers use a combination of these things. For instance, a quick page fix is usually done with just a text editor, whereas the creation of a table is better done with a WYSIWYG editor. It's important to understand the unique advantages each editor offers so that you can easily decide which tool will work best for the particular job you are doing. For more information on editors, consult Chapter 10.

■ **Text editors**—Text editors are the simplest tools for creating HTML files. All you have to do is type in the HTML, save it, and you're

13

finished. Text editors have become more sophisticated in the past few years. For instance, Notepad++ has a built-in HTML plug-in that colors your tags and does some text formatting to make it easier to create your pages (see Figure 13.1).

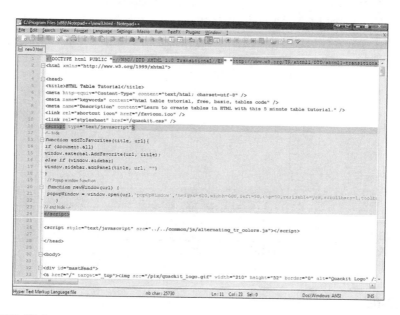

FIGURE 13.1

A web page seen in Notepad++.

■ **WYSIWYG editors**—These editors enable you to create web pages by working directly with the page, without having to bother with the HTML code. Your screen appears the same as it does in a browser, and the editor builds the HTML for you. WYSIWYG editors (see Figure 13.2) can be a huge time saver, but they can also lead to pages with proprietary tags or pages that don't display correctly in every browser.

Parts of a Page

So let's look at the tags and structures that make up the format of a web page. Understanding the parts of the page is invaluable in creating your own pages and learning from other people's web page code. This section covers those basic tags and a couple of other ways HTML pages can be structured (`<div>` tags, tables, frames, and layers).

13

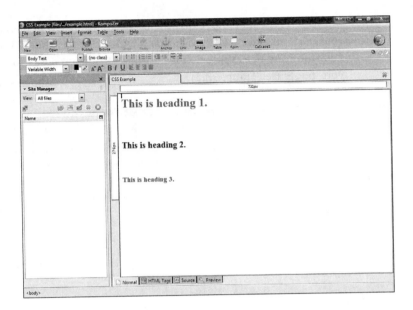

FIGURE 13.2
KompoZer is an open source WYSIWYG editor.

Basic Parts

There are some tags that every web page has to have:

- **<html></html>**—This tag says this is an HTML document. It is essential and comes at the beginning and end of an HTML document.

- **<head></head>**—This tag is for the heading part of the HTML file. Nothing that appears in the <head> tag appears in the body of your web page.

- **<title></title>**—This tag defines the title of the website as it appears in the title bar of the browser. The <title> tag appears within the <head> tag, so the text does not appear in the body of the web page.

- **<body></body>**—This is the main part of your web page. Everything in here is what shows up in the web browser.

So, put together properly, the HTML code looks like this:

```
<html>
    <head>
        <title>This is the title of this web page.</title>
    </head>
    <body>
        This is the body of the HTML document.
    </body>
</html>
```

Documenting Your Code with Comments

A good web developer documents his code. When developing a simple page, everything about it is easy to keep straight, but as your pages get more and more complicated, you need to add notes in the code to help you remember why you did certain things. Also, if you are working with other people on your web page, commenting lets them know what you did if they look at your code without your being present. To add notes, use the comment tag. The comment tag takes this form:

> **note** Notice how I have used indentation in this example to make sure the opening and closing tags line up. This is done with tabs and helps you keep your code straight.

```
<!--This is a comment-->
```

This text will never be displayed on the web page and serves only as a note to the web developer.

Tables

Tables are not only useful for storing information but also as a structural tool for design. Normally a table creates a grid of information like this:

Fruits	Sales
Apple	$15
Orange	$10

Tables are not always this simple, though. Some web developers use tables to structure their web pages. In fact, tables can be essential to properly spacing elements on websites. Tables can contain text, images, and other elements and can be nested within each other. Let's look at some simple examples.

13

First, based on the web page structures described earlier in this chapter (header, body, footer, and sidebars), a web page can be created with a table. The following HTML code produces a simple web page that uses tables:

```
<html>
    <head>
        <title>Sample Page using Tables</title>
    </head>
    <body>
        <table  border=1 cellspacing=0 cellpadding=0>
            <tr >
                <td width=73 valign=top>
                <br/>
                </td>
                <td width=168 valign=top>
                <br/>Header
                </td>
                <td width=84 valign=top>
                <br/>
                </td>
            </tr>
            <tr >
                <td width=73 valign=top>
                <br/>Sidebar 1
                </td>
                <td width=168 valign=top>
                <br/>Body
                </td>
                <td width=84 valign=top>
                <br/>Sidebar 2
                </td>
            </tr>
            <tr >
                <td width=73 valign=top>
                <br/>
                </td>
                <td width=168 valign=top>
                <br/>Footer
                </td>
                <td width=84 valign=top>
```

```
                    <br/>
                    </td>
                </tr>
            </table>
        </body>
    </html>
```

This table produces a simply structured web page (see Figure 13.3).

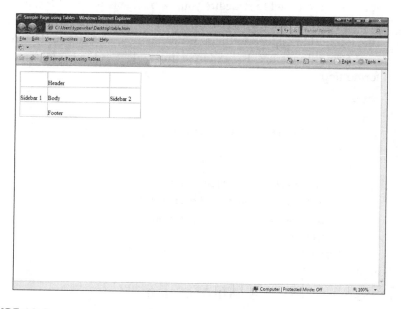

FIGURE 13.3

A page structured with a simple table.

If you add a bit more content, you retain the initial table structure and your content stays in place. Nesting tables is one way to do this. HTML enables you to create tables that nest within other tables. These tables within tables can give you even greater control over your content. So, for example, in the page shown in Figure 13.3, you could nest another table within the body section of the larger table to create structure within the body part of the table.

Nested tables are hard to code by hand and really should be left up to the HTML Jedi table masters. Your best bet is to use a WYSIWYG editor to help you create the table so you don't have to mess with the HTML code.

If you're brave enough and want to learn more about coding tables, consult the following sites:

- **W3Schools**—HTML Tables, www.w3schools.com/html/html_tables.asp
- **HTML Code Tutorial**—www.htmlcodetutorial.com/tables
- **Quackit.com**—HTML Table Tutorial, www.quackit.com/html/html_table_tutorial.cfm

`<div>` Tags

A common tag used to structure your web page is `<div>`. This tag acts as a divider for your web page sections. These divided sections can then have specific formatting applied to them, which gives you greater control over minute-level formatting issues. For example, this code uses the `<div>` tag for formatting:

```html
<html>
    <head>
        <title>Sample Page using DIV tags</title>
    </head>
    <body>
        <div style="text-align:center;">
        <h1>This is centered heading 1</h1>
        <p>This is a centered paragraph</p>
        </div>
    </body>
</html>
```

This code aligns the text to the center of the browser for all text in the `<div>` tag. It does not matter whether the text is a heading or just normal text. The preceding code produces the web page shown in Figure 13.4.

For some of the clearest and most complete information on the `<div>` tag, consult www.w3schools.com/tags/tag_DIV.asp.

Frames

Frames are another way to create structure on your page. Frames essentially create multiple web pages that are displayed within one web page. Just as a table

caution Theoretically, frames sound like an ideal way to create web pages; however, they've proven to be problematic and are generally seen as bad design and structure these days. Use tables, `<div>` tags, and cascading style sheets (or CSS—more on those to come) to achieve better results. Regardless, you should be aware of frames because other developers use them, but keep in mind that there are better ways to structure a page.

13

contains cells of content, a web page that uses frames is divided similarly, but each cell acts as a separate web page.

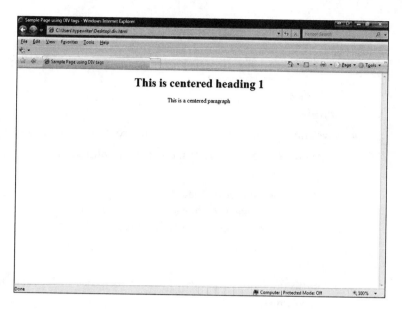

FIGURE 13.4

This is the web page that results from the code using <div> *tags.*

To use frames, you need to create several web pages and use a set of tags on one page to create a site that uses frames. The following instructions show you how to create a few pages and then create a single HTML document that displays them all at once. To create example web pages that use frames, follow these steps:

1. Create a web page containing this code:

```
<html>
    <head>
        <title>Frame1</title>
    </head>
    <body>
        This is frame 1
    </body>
</html>
```

2. Save this page as `frameone.html`.

3. Create a web page containing this code:

```
<html>
    <head>
        <title>Frame2</title>
    </head>
    <body>
        This is frame 2
    </body>
</html>
```

4. Save this page as `frametwo.html` in the same place as `frameone.html`.

5. Create a web page called `frames.html` containing this code:

```
<html>
        <frameset cols="90,*">
            <frame src ="frameone.html" />
            <frame src ="frametwo.html" />
        </frameset>
</html>
```

6. Save this page as `frames.html` in the same place as `frameone.html` and `frametwo.html`.

7. View `frames.html` in your browser (see Figure 13.5).

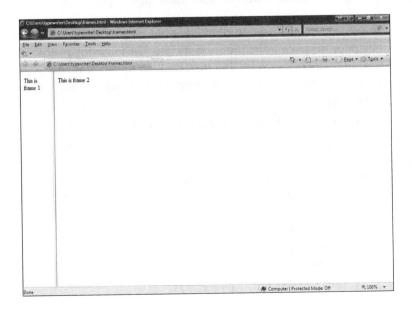

FIGURE 13.5

This sample web page uses frames.

Layers

The `<layers>` tag creates layers of web page elements that can be dynamically displayed and piled on top of each other. Imagine layers as stacks of pictures and documents on your desk. The top layer obscures the layers underneath. Like frames, this appears to be a good idea, but the `<layers>` tag does not work correctly in all browsers. This leads to problems because you don't know what browsers people will be using when they visit your site.

Cascading Style Sheets

A CSS is a file that contains the formatting for how HTML elements are displayed on any web page that refers to it. A CSS is a file that sits on the web server and contains that information. A CSS keeps your website organized, consistent, and much easier to maintain.

The word *cascading* might throw you off, but all it means is that the style sheet can control the formatting for your whole document from one place. Using a CSS means you have all the control in formatting down to a detailed level, or you can let the CSS take care of it. So, for example, if you want all your body text to be regular text, you can let the CSS define that, but if you have a single word that you want to italicize, you can still do that by using a tag around the text. There is a priority to formatting, which means that the formatting at the level closest to the code takes priority over formatting furthest from the code. The following list shows you the priority of formatting:

1. Browser default
2. External style sheet (CSS)
3. Internal formatting (in the `<head>` tag)
4. Specifically applied formatting

So, in the preceding list, because the italics is specifically applied (4), it overrides all the other formatting (1, 2, 3).

Format of a Style Sheet

The format of an external style sheet (separate file) or an internal one (contained in the HTML file) is the same. This can be in a separate style sheet or in the `<head>` tag of a particular web page. The format is simply

```
tag {property: value}
```

These are the different parts:

- **Tag**—This is the HTML tag to which you want to apply a tag.
- **Property**—This is the property (text color, size, or special formatting) of the text you want to apply to the tag.
- **Value**—This is the value of the property (red, bold, underlined) you want applied to the tag.

So, for example, if you want all <H1> tags to be red,

- **Tag**—h1
- **Property**—color
- **Value**—red

Put it together in code, and it looks like this:

```
h1 {color: red}
```

This changes all your <H1> tags so that the text is red. If you want the color to be blue instead, just change the reference to

```
h1 {color: blue}
```

All your <H1> heads are now blue.

Creating and Linking a Style Sheet

This section covers how to create the files and links in HTML documents to use a CSS. A linked style sheet enables you to control the formatting on multiple documents from a centralized place. If you are using a CSS to control the formatting on several pages and want to change all the pages at once, you just need to change the CSS.

To link to an external style sheet, you need to put a link in the <head> area of your web page. This link takes this structure:

```
<link rel="stylesheet" type="text/css" href="site.css" />
```

In this case, a link to a file (with the type of text/css) named site.css is the name of your CSS.

To practice creating a CSS, follow these steps:

1. Create a text file containing this code:

   ```
   h1 {
   color:red;
   }
   ```

```
h2 {
color:blue;
}

h3 {
color:green;
}
```

2. Save this page as `site.css`.

3. Create a web page called `example.html` containing this code:

```
<html>
    <head>
        <title>CSS Example</title>
        <link rel="stylesheet" type="text/css" href="site.css" />
    </head>
    <body>
        <h1>This is heading 1.<h1>
        <h2>This is heading 2.<h2>
        <h3>This is heading 3.<h3>
    </body>
</html>
```

4. Save this page as `example.html` in the same location as `site.css`.

5. Open `example.html` in a browser, and you will see colored text.

More Information on CSS

This is just a taste of how CSS works. You can get quite a bit more information on formatting and building complex web pages at the following websites:

■ **W3C School (www.w3schools.com/css/default.asp)**—This is one of the best tutorial sites on the Internet. Not only can you find an amazing CSS tutorial here, but many other tutorials, including HTML and JavaScript. Bookmark this site!

■ **The CSS Tutorial (www.csstutorial.net/)**—This is a clear, simple CSS tutorial.

■ **CSS Tutorial (www.echoecho.com/css.htm)**—This is a well written and complete CSS tutorial.

13

Scripting

Scripts are small pieces of code made from a few lines of text. Scripting is adding that programming code to a website. Scripting is more complex than HTML tags. Some examples are JavaScript, VBScript, and Perl. To some, scripting might seem like a scary word. You might be saying to yourself, "I don't know how to program." Using scripts within your HTML is by no means a cake walk, but it is also not impossible. A number of different scripting languages are used on the web (JavaScript, Perl, VBScript), and they can make your web pages fantastically interactive and fun. The keys when experimenting with scripting are to do your research, back up your work, and test as much as you can.

Here are some basic scripting resources on the Internet:

- **tizag.com**—This site has many tutorials for beginners. You can learn to script in JavaScript, PHP, Perl, Ajax, ASP, and VBScript.
- **Web-Wise-Wizard.com**—This site has an easy-to-follow JavaScript tutorial.
- **webmonkey.com**—As mentioned previously, this is a great beginner site brought to you by *Wired* magazine with excellent scripting tutorials.

Using Templates

Now that you understand how to create a web page with HTML, you'll probably be surprised to know that some sites offer website templates for free, complete with fully formed pages and CSS. I recommend starting with these templates but then applying what you've learned in this chapter to enhance your site. Web templates can save you a lot of time (and money), but they can also introduce complications that you don't need, such as formatting or images you don't like.

> **caution** Never pay for a website template. The Internet is full of sites that give away website templates.

13

How'd They Do That?

You've probably seen some incredible sites on the Internet and wondered how the web developer created a particular element of the site. This chapter covers what to do when you find something cool on another person's website and want to use it.

This chapter is not a guide to stealing other people's work. People work hard to build amazing Internet sites, and it would be unethical for you to steal their work and claim it as your own. But there are ways to learn how the web developer created the content, and by learning their methods, you can create your own spectacular content.

Viewing Code from Other Websites

If you find a website that has something on it that you like, you can always look at that website's code. There's nothing illegal or unethical about this. In fact, it's like opening the hood of a car and looking at how the engine works.

Any site on the Internet allows you to see the source code. To view a page's source, follow these steps:

1. Open a page in a browser.

2. From the View menu, choose Page Source. A page similar to that shown in Figure 14.1 appears.

FIGURE 14.1

The source view of a web page.

This displays the whole page's text and is useful if you want to see how the whole page is constructed. If you are interested in only a portion of the page, there are tools described later in this chapter to help with this.

Web Development Firefox Add-Ons

One of the great advantages of the Firefox browser is the opportunity to use add-ons. Several Firefox add-ons are available for web development. The

Firefox browser has been embraced by the web development community, and that community has created, and will keep creating, interesting add-ons for Firefox. These add-ons help you figure how other people's websites work.

To see how add-ons work, check out the Web Development section of the Firefox Add-ons page (https://addons.mozilla.org/en-US/firefox/browse/type:1/cat:4), as shown in Figure 14.2. This page lists the latest and greatest web development add-ons.

FIGURE 14.2

The Web Development section of the Firefox Add-Ons website.

Recommended Firefox Web Development Add-Ons

Here are some Firefox add-ons that I recommend. They'll come in handy as you develop your own site:

■ **Web Developer (https://addons.mozilla.org/en-US/firefox/ addon/60)**—This is one of my favorite add-ons. Developed by Chris Pederick, it adds a number of useful web development features to your Firefox (see Figure 14.3). These include allowing access to information about web pages, forms, and images. The add-on also has several validation functions and View Source options. You can access the features via a new toolbar and menus that show up on your Firefox browser after you have installed the plug-in.

14

FIGURE 14.3

A nice feature of the Web Developer add-on is highlighting all the headings on a web page.

■ **Page Validator (https://addons.mozilla.org/en-US/firefox/addon/ 2250)**—This add-on validates your web page according to the World Wide Web Consortium (W3C) standards.

■ **Firebug (https://addons.mozilla.org/en-US/firefox/addon/1843)**— Firebug integrates a script viewer into your Firefox window (see Figure 14.4). This enables you to view the source of a web page at the same time you are viewing it from the same browser. When you highlight elements in code, they are highlighted in the web page view. You can see the HTML code and the CSS code along with other more advanced views (scripts, DOM).

■ **IE Tab (https://addons.mozilla.org/en-US/firefox/addon/1419)**— This add-on enables you to display Internet Explorer tabs in a Firefox browser (see Figure 14.5). With it, you can see how your page will look in the two major browsers from inside Firefox.

■ **Screengrab! (https://addons.mozilla.org/en-US/firefox/addon/ 1146)**—If you want to get a screen shot of an entire web page, this add-on allows you to do just that.

FIGURE 14.4

Firebug enables you to see the script and the page at the same time.

FIGURE 14.5

With this add-on, you can view the IE version of a page from within Firefox.

14

■ **ColorZilla (https://addons.mozilla.org/en-US/firefox/addon/271)**—One of the things you need to do when designing a website is define your color scheme. ColorZilla, shown in Figure 14.6, identifies the colors that complement each other and look good with your message. ColorZilla enables you to click on a color item on any web page and obtain its color information and its color complements (what goes well with it).

FIGURE 14.6

Using ColorZilla's eye dropper in the lower left to determine the exact color of this picture.

■ **YSlow (https://addons.mozilla.org/en-US/firefox/addon/5369)**—Yahoo! has rules for high-performing websites (http://developer.yahoo.com/performance/index.html#rules). This add-on validates your page with these criteria in mind.

■ **MeasureIt (https://addons.mozilla.org/en-US/firefox/addon/539)**—If you have ever wondered what size an element on a web page is, this add-on enables you to see the exact size of elements in pixels (see Figure 14.7).

■ **CSSViewer (https://addons.mozilla.org/en-US/firefox/addon/2104)**—This add-on enables you to view a website's cascading style sheet.

Recommended Chrome Web Development Add-Ons

Google's Chrome browser has gained popularity in the past two years. It is fast, reliable, and extensible. Being newer to the game than Firefox, there are fewer add-ons for Chrome. Here are some of the better ones:

■ **Extensions for Web Developers (https://chrome.google.com/extensions/featured/web_dev)**—This is Google's list of add-ons for web developers. Nothing here is as excellent as Firebug, but there are a number of good choices.

14

FIGURE 14.7

Using MeasureIt enables you to see the size of this image.

■ **Speed Tracer (https://chrome.google.com/extensions/detail/
ognampngfcbddbfemdapefohjiobgbdl)**—This add-on shows you how
quickly your website loads, including the HTML, images, scripts, and
any advances features.

■ **Chrome Editor (https://chrome.google.com/extensions/detail/
nglgdmkkiemejlladcdjegcllaieegoe)**—This add-on allows you to edit
Hypertext Markup Language (HTML) scripts (both HTML 4 and 5),
Adobe Flash objects, and your cascading style sheet (CSS).

Recommended Safari Web Development Add-Ons

Apple computers are the most common choice of professional web developers.
The Safari browser comes pre-installed with any Apple operating system so
you may be using Safari as one of your main web browsers. Here are a few of
the best add-ons:

■ **Safari Dev Center (http://developer.apple.com/safari/)**—This page
hosts Apple's latest Safari development tools. It also includes useful
videos, sample code and a nifty reference library. This is certainly the
place to get the official Apple development information.

14

- **Safari Reference Library (http://developer.apple.com/safari/ library/documentation/AppleApplications/Conceptual/Safari_ Developer_Guide/1Introduction/Introduction.html)**—This is the developer tool section of the reference library mentioned above. It contains clear and complete information on developing with the safari browser.

- **Mac Developer Tips (http://macdevelopertips.com/)**—This blog does what is says by offering tips, tools, and code for developers working on Macs.

Badges

When I hear the word "badges," I immediately think about Boy Scouts. As a Boy Scout, I tried to get as many badges as I could with an almost fanatical devotion. Websites can have badges, too. A website badge is simply a small piece of code and graphic you put on your website to show affiliation with another website. It is like a small, graphical hyperlink.

There are literally thousands of web badges. You can get them from the originating websites or from badge sites such as Zwahlen Design (www.zwahlendesign.ch/en/node/19), which not only gives you hundreds of badges but shows you how to make your own (see Figure 14.8).

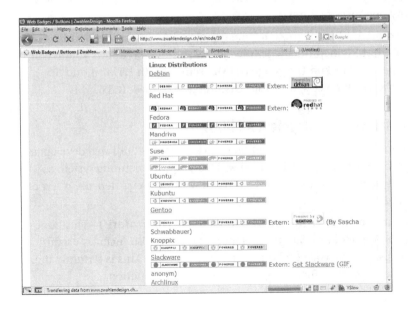

FIGURE 14.8

Some of the badges on the Zwahlen Design site.

14

You add a badge to your website to show affiliation. So if you have a WordPress site or use MySQL, it is a nice thing for you to add a badge for those things. There are two things to keep in mind with badges. First, don't overwhelm your site with gaudy or large badges. This is the equivalent of wearing ostentatious jewelry. Second, don't overwhelm your visitors with a huge number of badges. Having too many badges on your website is like having too many Christmas lights on your house. Don't be that house, and don't be that website.

With Web 2.0 websites, there are new kinds of badges that actually contain content. For example, if you have a Twitter account, you might want to add the Twitter badge on your site (see Figure 14.9). Twitter is a microblogging website that lets you blog 140 characters at a time. If you have the Twitter badge, when you post to Twitter, the content automatically shows up on your Twitter badge.

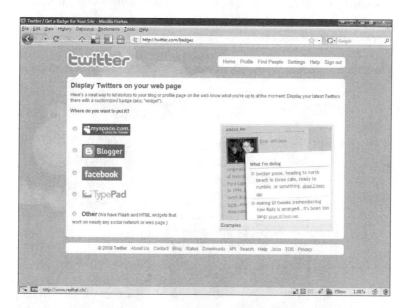

FIGURE 14.9

Add Twitter badges through this part of the website (http://twitter.com/badges).

Most of the Web 2.0 websites will tell you how to add one of these more complicated badges.

Templates

You can also find website and web page templates on the Internet. These are pre-designed web pages that you customize with your content. Again, there are millions of these on the Internet, covering a wide range of color schemes and content types. There are generally two categories of free web templates: generic templates and application-specific templates.

Generic templates are website or web page templates that you can use with any website creation tool (see Figure 14.10). They usually just contain the basic HTML file and some basic graphics. The easiest way to find these templates is to Google `free web page template` or `free website template`.

caution Do not, under any circumstances, pay for web templates you find on the Internet. First, there are millions of free ones that you can download and use on your site. Second, trust in your own creativity. By modifying an existing free template, you may be able to create exactly what you need for your website.

FIGURE 14.10

This website offers free web page templates.

14

If you are using a specific program to create a web page, you might want to search on the Internet for templates specific to your application. Just add the name of your application to the search terms mentioned in the preceding paragraph to find application-specific templates.

> **note** I certainly spend a good portion of this book telling you how much great stuff you can get on the web for free. You definitely can find quality templates on the Internet for free, but you will have to sift through a lot of things to find what you are looking for. Be patient; you might not find what you are looking for right away.

Developer Networks and Sites

If there are millions of websites on the Internet, there must be a lot of people developing those websites. These people like to talk to each other. This socializing is good for more than just finding friends. It can be excellent for networking ideas and information about website developments.

Developer network sites are websites where you can find a solution to a problem or question you might have regarding web development. You can be assured that you will find someone willing to share their solution or ideas with you. Connecting to other web developers in these communities enables you to share your experiences. These folks obviously have something in common with you (they are also developing websites), so do your part and share your knowledge as well. Here are some of the best web developer networks:

- **Webmonkey (www.webmonkey.com/)**—Webmonkey was one of the first and best websites dedicated to website developers and setting up a community (see Figure 14.11). It was launched in 1999 by the folks who bring you *Wired* magazine but closed three short years later. But wait—Webmonkey has returned! The site was relaunched in 2008 and contains excellent tutorials, references, and a code library. There is a sense of fun and community on this site, and it continues to be an invaluable resource for web developers.

- **Yahoo! Developer Network (http://developer.yahoo.com/)**—This site is for people using Yahoo! technologies to develop websites and other applications. Although it might not have a direct impact on your website, if you are doing anything related to Yahoo!, you might want to check it out.

- **Google Groups (http://groups.google.com/)**—Google Groups are social connections that are based on interests. That could be anything from car racing to web development. Have a look around this site for web developer groups.

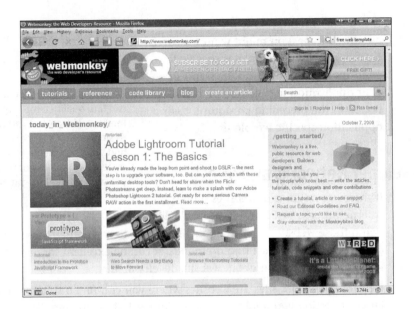

FIGURE 14.11
The relaunched Webmonkey.com.

> ▓ **Other Developer Sites and Groups**—If you are doing anything on the
> web or using a specific program to do web development, there is proba-
> bly a community on the web for that type of development.

Making Your Site Mobile

Being mobile means that you have access to the Internet away from your home or office, with a computer, cell phone, or PDA, and without the use of wires to connect. Mobile access is the fastest growing area of web development. If you've ever used your cell phone to look up directions, you have used the mobile web. Wireless technology has increased in prevalence because the hardware required to operate wireless technology has become smaller and faster. More and more people are using their phones and other devices to access the mobile web than ever before. As a web designer, you need to be aware of how the mobile web works and how your website might need to be changed to be used with the mobile web.

This chapter covers some of the most common mobile web devices and software. Then it covers what can and can't be done on the mobile web, and finally, how to make your website mobile compatible.

Why Should You Care About the Mobile Web?

Would someone walking down the street or driving in a car be interested in the information offered on your website? You might not think so, but consider these situations:

■ Someone standing in a knitting store, trying to decide which needle to buy, can access a knitting website to see what it recommends.

■ Someone trying to locate a particular item in a local store can find an image of the item online, through a site that sells the item, and use the phone or PDA to show it to the store clerk.

■ Someone with a taste for cannoli can use his cell phone or PDA to search for local Italian restaurants that have posted their menus to the web and offer cannoli.

As these examples illustrate, websites that cater to the mobile market will see traffic increase.

How People Access the Mobile Web

If you want to use the mobile web, you first need a device that provides a connection to the Internet. A cell phone, PDA, or wireless laptop would work. Then you use a browser built in to your device to go to an address, similar to the browser you use on your computer to access the Internet.

Mobile web devices can access almost any web page, but some pages are specifically designed for mobile web users. These pages display better and load faster on mobile devices.

Become a Mobile Web User

To be an effective developer of websites that are accessed by mobile web devices, you should be a mobile web user yourself.

Check to see whether your cell phone or personal digital assistant (PDA) accesses the mobile web. If you don't have one, try to get access to one so you can see what websites look like on these devices. If you are building sites specifically designed to be accessed by the mobile web, it is important to have a mobile web device on which to test your website.

For more information, see the following websites:

■ **Mobile Web Wikipedia Entry**—http://en.wikipedia.org/wiki/ Mobile_Web

- W3C Mobile Web Initiative—www.w3.org/Mobile/
- Mobile Web Best Practices 1.0—www.w3.org/TR/mobile-bp/

Mobile Web Devices (MWD)

At one time, computers used to fill whole rooms. They used vacuum tubes and punch cards to run complex calculations that helped book air travel and build the atomic bomb. Things have changed. Today, devices such as cell phones and PDAs are many times faster and much, much smaller. To understand how to use the mobile web to your website's advantage, it is important to know the tools available. Let's explore some of these devices and how they work.

Smartphones

We definitely can see that times are changing in the phone arena. No longer does a telephone need to be connected to the telephone network through wires from your house to a central switching office. Go to a college campus, and just count the number of cell phones you can see. We are no longer tied down to the phones on our desks.

We do more with our phones than ever before, and they are becoming indispensible. We can listen to music, take pictures, and even connect to the mobile web. Don't ignore this fast-growing market, because more people connect to the web via a smartphone than a computer.

PDAs

Along with the rise in cell phones, the early 1990s saw the introduction of handheld data devices. The air around you is being filled with data being sent to and from PDAs. Do you know someone with a portable email device such as a BlackBerry? Using one of those involves connecting to the mobile web.

Tablets and E-Readers

A new mobile web market involves tablet PCs and e-readers. The Apple iPad and Amazon Kindle are the most successful, but every hardware manufacturer is working on one of these devices.

Other Devices

Mobile devices are not limited to what you can carry around in your pocket. There are small mobile devices that users carry around or use in their cars. More and more, we are going to see web access on things we would never expect. Now a refrigerator can have a screen on it. If it can have a screen, you might be able to access the mobile web with it.

Mobile Operating Systems

Just as your desktop or laptop computer has an operating system—Windows, OSX, Linux, and so on—most mobile web devices have their own operating system. You should be familiar with a few major ones:

- **Apple iOS (www.apple.com/iphone/ios4/)**—The iPhone and iPad use this operating system. Like all Apple operating systems, the Apple iOS is easy to use and robust. It is also closed off and hard to manipulate.

- **Microsoft Windows Mobile (www.microsoft.com/windowsmobile/)**— This is a version of Microsoft Windows designed specifically to run on mobile devices (see Figure 15.1). It allows you to access familiar programs such as Microsoft Word and Microsoft Excel. It also comes standard with a version of Microsoft Internet Explorer.

FIGURE 15.1

Windows Mobile is for phones.

■ **Symbian (www.symbian.org/)**—This is an open-source mobile operating system used on phones from Fujitsu, LG, Mitsubishi, Motorola, Nokia, Samsung, Sharp, and Sony Ericsson. Symbian uses the Opera open-source mobile browser to access the mobile web.

■ **Android (http://code.google.com/android/)**—Android is Google's new operating system for mobile devices (see Figure 15.2). Like other Google projects, Android is an open-source operating system and development platform for handsets. Android uses its own embedded browser but encourages existing browser developers to develop versions of their web browser for Android-enabled devices.

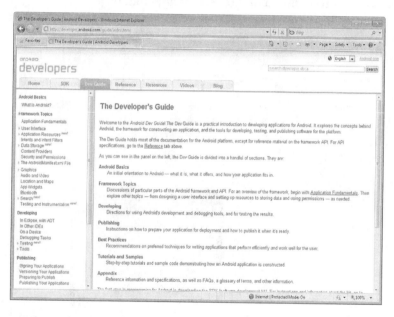

FIGURE 15.2

Google Android.

Mobile Browsers

Just as your desktop or laptop computer uses a web browser—Internet Explorer, Firefox, Safari, and so on—to access the Internet, mobile devices use similar browsers to access the mobile web. These browsers are different, though, and may not look like any browser you have ever seen:

- **Windows Internet Explorer Mobile (www.microsoft.com/ windowsmobile/en-us/downloads/microsoft/internet-explorer-mobile.mspx)**—This is a web browser that comes installed with Windows mobile devices. It has several viewing options, and you can sync your Favorites list with your PC.

- **Safari (www.apple.com/iphone/features/safari.html)**—This is a version of the Safari browser that comes installed on Apple's iPhone (see Figure 15.3). It allows eight windows to be open at once and is fully integrated into the rest of the iPhone operating system. If you get a text message on your iPhone and it has a web address, if you touch the screen, the Safari browser displays that page.

FIGURE 15.3
The Safari browser for the iPhone.

- **Opera (www.opera.com/products/mobile/)**—The mobile Opera browser is an open-source browser for smartphones, including the iPhone, and PDAs. Since it was created, it has been installed and runs on millions of phones. It's the default browser with the Symbian mobile operating system.

■ **Skyfire (www.skyfire.com)**—Another competitor in the mobile browser market is Skyfire. Currently, there is a Windows mobile, Android, and Symbia version. It plays Flash video, content recommendation and social sharing options.

For more up-to-date information, look at the Wikipedia entry on mobile browsers: http://en.wikipedia.org/wiki/Mobile_browser.

Limitations of the Mobile Web

The mobile web gives access to the Internet from anywhere, with devices that are small and lightweight. There's no doubt about it: the mobile web is probably the best thing since sliced bread. But the mobile web has some limitations that you must be aware of before you create or modify your website for it:

■ **Speed**—The speed of the mobile web is not the same as what you get with conventional methods of connection. Even with the fastest Wi-Fi connections, some mobile devices have processors and graphics engines that are slower than a typical desktop or laptop computer. Although mobile broadband carriers want to impress you with the speed of their 3 and 4G networks, they are still much slower than home PC connections.

■ **Screen size and resolution**—Mobile devices have small screens with low resolutions and limited aspect ratios.

■ **Lack of web applications**—Not everything that can run on the web can run on the mobile web. Most mobile web browsers can't run JavaScript or Flash applications, making some content inaccessible.

■ **Page sizes**—If your website is designed with a fixed width or length, it might not be displayed correctly on the mobile web. If you are thinking about a mobile website, pay close attention to your page sizes.

Making Your Website Mobile

I'm going to show you how to create web pages that work best on the mobile web and how to test these websites. As with any website, you should follow the steps of planning, designing, building, and then testing. This section covers topics in those areas specific to the mobile web.

Mobile Browser Detection

When people come to your website using a mobile web device, you might want to direct them to a particular part of your website. Detecting a mobile web user might not be as easy as it seems. There are scripts in languages such as PHP that can detect a mobile web browser and direct the visitor to a more mobile-friendly part of your website. If you are serious about detecting and redirecting mobile users, look at the following locations:

- **How to Redirect Mobile Phones and Handhelds to Your Mobile Website**—www.stepforth.com/resources/web-marketing-knowledge-base/redirect-mobile-iphone-visitors-mobile-content/

- **Detecting Mobile Browsers**—www.brainhandles.com/techno-thoughts/detecting-mobile-browsers

- **Detecting and Automatically Redirecting Website Visitors**—http://studiohyperset.wordpress.com/2006/10/06/detecting-and-automatically-redirecting-website-visitors-who-visit-a-standard-webpage-website-on-mobile-handheld-wireless-pda-or-cel-cell-phone-devices-browsers-to-a-mobile-version-of-the-webpage-or-w/

Domains and Subdomains

You might not want your whole site accessible to the mobile web, or you might want to create a website specifically for the mobile web. If you are creating a website specifically for the mobile web user, you might want to create a specific domain or subdomain. Here are some examples of mobile web–specific domains:

- `m.` **Prefix**—If you go to a mobile website, it might have a subdomain suffix of `m.`. For example, the mobile version of Google is `m.google.com`, and the mobile version of cnn.com is `m.cnn.com`. Because most host providers don't charge for new subdomains, this is usually a free option.

- `.mobi`—There is now a high-level domain for mobile phones, known as `.mobi`. This domain was set up specifically to be used with mobile web content. This domain was sponsored by major telecommunications and software companies to separate their sites from other domains.

Use the Right Code

You can use HTML to create mobile websites, but you might want to use other languages specifically designed to make mobile web pages as easy to use as possible. Here are a couple of options:

- **Wireless Markup Language**—An early version of a language specifically for mobile devices

- **XHTML**—A markup language (like HTML) that allows web pages to work better on some mobile web browsers

Page Sizes

Mobile web browsers have small screens, and you want to provide as much information as possible on that screen. Don't have a huge image or header text at the top of your page, or you're asking people to scroll down immediately.

Interface

When designing web pages for mobile web browsers, keep in mind that the interface design might be completely different from that of a regular web page:

- **Shortcuts**—Make sure to use lots of shortcuts. On a mobile device, it is easier to select a shortcut than to scroll.

- **Vertical scrolling**—This is not the easiest thing to do with some mobile web devices. Keep vertical scrolling to a minimum.

- **Horizontal scrolling**—Scrolling across the screen should be avoided at all costs. Some browsers don't even allow this function.

- **Images**—Images are big files that introduce display problems, so keep images to a minimum. If you have to add images, try to keep them under 100×100 pixels.

- **Text**—Keep your text and text size as small as you can. Remember that some mobile web users might be paying to download your page.

15

Things to Avoid

Some things that you might use on a standard web page should be avoided at all costs for a mobile web page. These things can cause the page to display incorrectly or not at all. If at all possible, avoid these web features:

- Tables
- Frames
- Pop-ups

Mobile Web Tools and Sites

There is a growing community of online mobile web developers. If you are going to be developing mobile websites, I recommend that you visit these sites and take part in the communities:

- **A Beginner's Guide to Mobile Web Development (http://mobiforge. com/starting/story/a-beginners-guide-mobile-web-development)**—An excellent spot to begin learning about mobile web development.

- **Mobile Web Best Practices 1.0 (www.w3.org/TR/2005/WD-mobile-bp-20051220/)**—The W3C not only creates standards for regular websites, it issues mobile web best practices. Familiarize yourself with these if you are going to do more mobile web development.

- **Mobile Web Site Builders (www.site.mobi & www.mobisitegalore.com/)**—These sites enable you to create simple mobile websites that meet mobile standards.

- **mobiForge (http://mobiforge.com/)**—A mobile web developer's website with designing, development, and testing resources (see Figure 15.4).

- **W3C Mobile Web Initiative (www.w3.org/Mobile/)**—W3C's home for mobile web page development.

- **Preparing Your Web Content for iPad (http://developer.apple.com/safari/library/technotes/tn2010/tn2262/index.html)**—The page covers Apple's safari browser on the iPad.

- **iPad Web Development Tips (www.nczonline.net/blog/2010/04/06/ipad-web-development-tips/)**—This page covers iPad-specific coding practices.

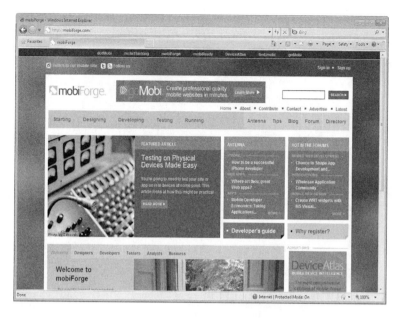

FIGURE 15.4

mobiForge is an excellent development site for the mobile web.

Testing Your Site on a Mobile Phone

One of the unique features of developing for the mobile web is testing your web page on different devices. The good news is that you don't have to go out and buy all the mobile devices you can find and check your page on them. There are websites that can evaluate your mobile website and emulate what it will look like on different mobile devices. Here are some to consider:

- **mobiReady (http://ready.mobi/)**—This is an evaluation tool for mobile websites that checks a particular page or an entire website for how well it will work on mobile devices. This site is a must to test your mobile web page.

- **Mobile Emulator (http://mtld.mobi/emulator.php)**—This site tests how your web page would function on different mobile devices.

- **Testing on Mobile Devices Using Emulators (www.klauskomenda.com/archives/2008/03/17/testing-on-mobile-devices-using-emulators/)**—A great article that covers the emulator process and links to some great emulators.

Site Testing and Maintenance

Testing Your Website

By now you have probably spent hours on your website. You have let your creative juices flow, and now you can't wait to share the site with someone. So you proudly send your uniform resource locator (URL) to a friend, who looks at the website and comments on only the broken links and missing images. You were expecting her to say how cool your work was, but instead she only noticed what you did wrong. This is definitely not the reaction you wanted. To stop this from happening, you need to test your website before showing it to other people.

When you test your website, you simply go over the work you have done and make sure it is correct. Testing can involve simple things, such as making sure your links work, to more complex things, such as optimizing your HTML code. This chapter gives you some guidelines on what to test as well as some free resources and tools you can use.

16

Why Testing Is Important

Nothing is more frustrating than going to a website and finding links that don't work or images that are missing. How many times have you clicked on a link and been presented with *the dreaded 404 error*?

Broken links say a lot about a web designer's work. When you come across a 404 error on the website, you might think any of the following:

Geek Speak

The dreaded 404 error

When a web browser can't find a page to which a link refers, the browser displays an error page. This is HTTP Error Code 404—File Not Found, sometimes referred to as a dead link (see Figure 16.1). This error is the result of inadequate testing.

- This website is old and forgotten.
- This web designer doesn't care about broken links.
- This web designer did not check his work.
- This web designer doesn't know what he is doing.

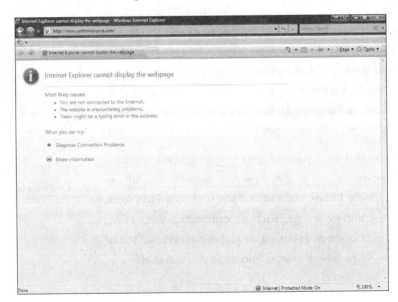

FIGURE 16.1
This is an example of a 404—File Not Found error.

You don't want people to think these things about you or your website. You want them to come to your site for the content and not let mistakes or broken links get in the way. Nothing is more embarrassing than when someone emails you about a problem with your website. It's worse only if no one tells you about the error.

If you're developing a website for a business or an organization, it's especially important to test the site thoroughly so that the business or organization doesn't look bad.

A well-tested website makes everyone involved look good. When all your links are working, your images are showing up, and your site is loading correctly in multiple browsers, you can be pleased knowing that your visitors will have a great experience.

Building a Test Plan

A test plan is a list of the things you are going to test before releasing your website. It might be just a list you create for yourself in a Word file, or it might be something more elaborate that your boss or clients want to see. If you are building websites for other people, it is essential that you write up a formal test plan.

You need to think about several things as you create your test plan. "Do all my links work correctly?" is just one question in what can be an overwhelming list of things to test. Your test plan is probably going to go through some changes. Keep a list of things to test for as you are developing your site, and it will be easier for you to remember everything when it comes time to test.

Start at the End

I always begin by defining what must work on the website before I can release it. Start at the end by deciding what must work, and then work backward. Think of it like starting a journey—you need to know where you are going before you can decide how to get there. For example, the page must load correctly in the major browsers. If this is not the case, you are not finished developing the website. If the page loads correctly, you can cross that off the list and move on to the next test. Defining the minimum necessary to be correct before you can call the website done helps you know when you can release it.

Testing Basic Functionality

For any website to be called finished, it must have some level of basic functionality. This includes simple things, such as making sure the text looks right and is spelled correctly, to making sure your Hypertext Markup Language (HTML) forms and Hypertext Preprocessor (PHP) scripts work correctly.

Basically, do all the things that are supposed to work actually work? At a minimum, these are the things you need to check on a website:

Functionality

- All links go to correct pages
    - Internal links
    - External links (links to other websites)
    - Email links
    - No 404 errors
- All forms work correctly
    - Form captures the right data
    - Form hides passwords
    - Form buttons function correctly
    - Form results stored correctly
- Page displays properly in all major browsers
    - Check major browsers at different resolutions (see the later section titled "Testing Browsers")
- All graphic files display properly
    - No missing graphics icons
    - Graphics look good at different resolutions and depths of color

Content

- Text and graphics are clear and readable
- Text is spelled correctly and is grammatically correct
- The most important text is the most prominent

Testing HTML

HTML is an amazing language that has changed the online world. One of the great features of HTML is that, by and large, it works the same for all browsers. Credit for this goes to the World Wide Web Consortium (W3C). This is a group whose goal is to bring the web to its full potential and act as a gatekeeper of changes to HTML. The W3C offers a number of useful tools to help you validate your HTML. These tools are great, but the W3C's standards are incredibly high. It is difficult, if not impossible, to find a website with which the W3C's tools can't find a problem. Don't worry: Use the W3C's validation tool to catch the obvious problems, and don't sweat the super small stuff.

To use the HTML Validator, follow these steps:

1. Go to http://validator.w3.org/ (see Figure 16.2).

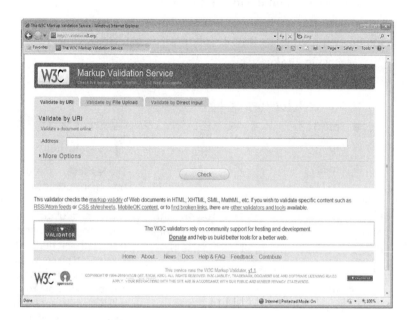

FIGURE 16.2

The W3C Markup Validation Service web page is a useful and free tool.

2. Enter your website address in the Address field.

3. Click Check.

The Validator then checks your web page and returns a report with errors or warnings. As I said before, the Validator is probably going to find tons of things "wrong" with your page. Read the report carefully, and evaluate whether the errors and warnings are really important. Some errors are major, such as HTML problems you might not have caught, whereas others are minor. Review the results, and use the Validator again whenever you make substantial changes to your website.

Testing Browsers

Not everyone on the web uses the same browser. Whenever one browser seems to have a dominant lead on the market, another one comes along. In the early 90s, this became a big problem with web developers because all the browsers began using their own HTML tags and interpreting standard tags in different ways. This means that if you are serious about testing your website, you need to test it on the major browsers.

To test your site on different browsers, you should have the latest versions of the following browsers installed so that you can check your website on them:

- Mozilla Firefox
- Chrome
- Microsoft Internet Explorer
- Safari
- Opera
- Flock

Keep in mind that some browsers read HTML differently than others. You should always pay attention to a couple of things when checking other browsers. (They have all caused problems in the past.)

- Tables
- Lists
- Forms
- Scripts

Geek Speak

resolution

The *resolution* of your screen is how many pixels wide or tall it is. Your screen can't change size, but the number of pixels displayed can change. For example, your resolution might be 1024 pixels×768 pixels, whereas mine is 1680×1250. My screen has a higher resolution. Your website will look different on my screen than it does on yours.

Testing Resolution

Just because you have your computer set at one resolution doesn't mean that everyone has the same resolution. Testing your website at different resolutions shows you how other people can see your website.

Do not design with only your own resolution in mind. It is common for new website designers to think everyone has resolution settings that are the same as those on the developer's computer. This could not be further from the truth. In the early days of the web, you could depend on people having 800×600 or 1024×768 resolutions, but now with fancy plasma wide-screen monitors, the list of resolutions in use has grown. Graphics, text, and tables can look very different at different resolutions.

You can test resolutions in a couple of ways:

- **Change your own resolution**—One way to see how other people see your site at different resolutions is to change the resolution of your monitor and look at your site. This works well but becomes tedious.

■ **Use a web tool**—Several websites can help you see the resolution on different browsers. The best of these is called Browser Shots (http://browsershots.org/). In just a few minutes, you can get images of a website on dozens of browsers at almost as many resolutions and color depths (see Figure 16.3). Browser Shots shows you only pictures, but seeing images can point out problem areas that might show up on other browsers.

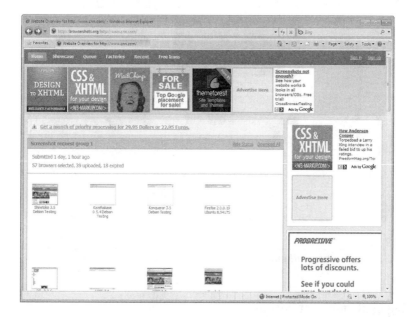

FIGURE 16.3

Browser Shots showing several different views of the same web page on different browsers.

Testing Printing

If a particular part of your website is intended to be printed—something like a map or form—make sure you test it on several printers to see how the printed page looks.

Testing Navigation

How a visitor navigates around the pages of your website is part of its usability. You need clear markers of where visitors currently are in the website; where they can go; and standard, easy-to-understand navigational elements on each page. It's important that all your pages have consistent elements so your visitors don't get lost in a mess of inconsistent web pages (see Figure 16.4).

FIGURE 16.4
Menus like this are navigational elements on a website.

Testing Consistency of Design

Along with consistent navigational elements, you need to make sure your website is graphically consistent. Each page should look similar to all the others. This doesn't mean all your pages need to be identical, but they should share visual elements, such as font, color, and arrangement.

One thing you might think of doing is making a template for each page. A template is just a model for the look and design of each page that you fill with different content. Templates can range from complex to simple. To learn how to use templates for your site, refer to Chapter 13, "Building a Site Using HTML."

For more advanced web designers, testing consistency of design means testing that your cascading style sheet (CSS) is working properly and the styles are applied to the appropriate text. For more information on using CSS, see Chapter 13.

Testing Security

Your website's security is worth worrying about. You might have created a simple website for your family photos and don't think you have anything worth worrying about, but a web vandal could gain access to your site and destroy it, or worse, use your website as a base to destroy other websites or gain access to your personal computer.

The best place to start checking security is with your hosting provider. You might want to ask your server provider whether it offers 128-bit security, spam protection, firewall protection, or something like ModSecurity (www.modsecurity.org/), an open-source web application firewall.

If you are using something like Google Sites, your website's security is handled by some of the best security on the web, so you have to worry more about spam than high security risks, but if you are running a business site that collects credit card information, you need to be especially concerned with security. Check with your hosting provider about how it ensures your website's security.

Next, read up on website security testing. Several excellent websites can help with this, including these:

■ **Open Web Application Security Project (OWASP)**—www.owasp.org

■ **The World Wide Web Security FAQ**—www.w3.org/Security/Faq

■ **W3C Security Resources**—www.w3.org/Security/security-resource

Testing Mobile Web

As mentioned in the previous chapter, it is important to test your website on mobile devices. Even if you have not thought about mobile access to your website, people will try to connect to it using mobile browsers. Here are some sites and tools to help you test your mobile website:

■ **Testing Mobile Web Sites Using Firefox (http://mobiforge.com/testing/story/testing-mobile-web-sites-using-firefox)**—An excellent source on using the Firefox browser to test mobile websites.

■ **W3C mobileOK Checker (http://validator.w3.org/mobile/)**—WC3 also provides a website checker for mobile sites. Remember this site will give you a large number of errors. Be sure to read the reporting detail before changing your site.

■ **mobiReady (http://ready.mobi/launch.jsp?locale=en_EN)**—mobi offers a mobile testing tool that checks whether your website meets mobile readiness standards and follows best practices.

Testing Accessibility

Unless you are creating a website especially for people with impaired vision, you might not be concerned about how accessible the website is to handicapped folks. The American Federation of the Blind suggests ways in which you can improve the accessibility of your website, such as these:

- Labeling graphics and images
- Labeling links
- Viewing your site without graphics

(Source: www.afb.org/Section.asp?SectionID=57&TopicID=167&DocumentID=2176.)

Also, you might want to make sure your site is accessible to the color blind. For more information about making your site color-blind accessible, see Chapter 11, "Working with Images."

After Testing

Testing is an ongoing process that you really can't finish, but you can come to a point where you think about letting other people see your creation. Remember, you are never going to get all the errors all the time. Fix what you can as quickly as possible and move on. Don't let a single error derail your website project.

Also, learn from your mistakes. Figure out what went wrong, and then apply it to the rest of the site or sites you are working on.

Testing Tools

You can use a number of tools to test your website, ranging from the simple tools mentioned already in this chapter to the following more complex tools:

- **HTML Tidy**—This is another great tool from the folks at W3C. HTML Tidy offers you ways to make sure your HTML is as clean and efficient as possible. The tool goes through all your HTML code and makes suggestions. It checks for connecting tags and orphan code.
  - **HTML Tidy site**—www.w3.org/People/Raggett/tidy/
  - **HTML Tidy online version tool**—http://infohound.net/tidy/

- **UITest.com Web Development Tools**—This is a set of tools to help you automatically test your website. This includes accessibility, browsers, coloring, and a site check.

  - **UITest.com Web Development Tools site**—http://uitest.com/

- **Dead-Links.com Free Broken Link Checker**—This site checks your website for broken links. It's a good, fast tool for checking for broken links.

  - **Dead-Links.com site**—www.dead-links.com/

16

Promoting Your Website

Whether your website is a small company website or a national charity, you should promote it to increase traffic. The more people who come to your website, the more people hear your message. The problem is that there are millions of websites out there. You have to do some work to promote yours.

Promoting your website can be simple or complex. If you are made of money, you can hire an ad agency to plaster your URL on billboards all over the world. I'm guessing that if you picked up this book, you are most likely looking to keep costs to a minimum.

This chapter is separated into two parts. The first part covers things you can do to promote your own website. This includes ways to publicize your URL and connect to others. The second section of the chapter covers what a search engine is and how it works. Then I'll tell you how to optimize your site to get the best search engine results.

Self-Promotion

When you promote your website, you're acting as your own advertising firm. People won't know anything about your website unless you tell them. Whether you use a sandwich board and walk up and down the streets or put your URL on a business card, marketing your website increases your exposure and ensures that more people will visit your site. In this section, I want to give you some ideas for how to promote your website's URL for free.

caution Beware of snake oil salesmen! As soon as your website gets noticed by enough people, you might begin to have people telling you how to promote your site and offering to sell you marketing services or documents that they guarantee will drive traffic to your site. Don't fall for this. You can find all the information about promoting your website for free on the web.

Have Excellent and Unique Content

The most important way to ensure regular traffic to your website is to have the highest quality, unique content. You must set your website apart from millions of others. The easiest way to do this is to trust your own voice and fill your website with the things that interest you.

If you have a website that is about making scrapbooks about kids involved in sports, make the best site you can about that. This can include showing the best examples you can find, reviewing products, or offering how-to tutorials.

On the other hand, a website that is just rehashed, boring, dull material or, worst of all, devoid of content altogether, will not attract visitors (see Figure 17.1). Try not to make your website only about you and how great you are. People want to find out about new things, not just about you.

Update Content

Having excellent content is the first part of the process of updating content. I cannot stress this enough. Ensuring there is fresh and interesting content on your website is the second part of the process. When you update content, give visitors who have already been to your site a reason to return. If people come back to your site and nothing has changed, you are not giving them a reason to return.

Update your content as much as you can, but don't fill your website with fluff or content that can be found anywhere. Instead, infuse new content with your personality and input.

FIGURE 17.1
The world's most boring web page.

Publicize Your URL

The easiest way for you to get the word out about your website is to publicize your URL. This means having your website address visible to people in ways that make them want to come to your site.

An easy way to promote your website is to include the URL on any material you send out. Suppose you have created a website for your cafe. Put the URL on the menu and any coupons you send out. Add the URL to your logo. If you send emails, add your URL to your *signature file.*

Also, if your content and website warrant it, you might want to create a regular newsletter announcing changes to content and any other important details. If you decide to do this, send email only to those people who ask for it so you are not accused of sending out spam.

Geek Speak

signature file

A signature file is a small bit of text that is automatically added to your email. It typically includes your name, contact information, and affiliated websites. The key to a good signature file is brevity, so include only important things. You can check the email program you are using to see how to include a signature file with your emails.

You will benefit here if you choose a small, easy-to-remember URL so that it does not confuse visitors or take over your posters.

Connect with Others

You can also promote your website by connecting to other people. Increasing the connections you have on- and offline enables you to share the work you have done with many other people. Remember, you don't know all the people your friends know, so the number of people who get your message grows as you meet and contact others.

caution Publicizing your URL does not mean knocking people over the head with it. It does not mean driving your car around with speakers on the back screaming your URL to anyone who will listen. Try to publicize, but not bully or overwhelm, with your message.

Linking to Others

The easiest way to make friends using your website is to link to other websites. Essentially, you put a link to someone else's website on your own site. This connects your site to other websites and makes it part of their network. When I link to a new site, I usually drop that site an email and let the person know I love what he is doing and that I have linked to him. I never ask that site owner to link back to me, but I do ask him to visit my site to take a look around.

Requesting Links

Requesting links means asking someone to put a link on his site to your site. Because it involves asking a complete stranger to do something, I tend not to do it. There may be special circumstances where this might be feasible, but they are uncommon. An example of a special circumstance would be a website within a specialized community. Say you have a board gaming website. You may want to connect with other board game sites and ask them to link to you. Just be polite and honest. In the end, the best advice is to link to others' sites and in turn, others will link to you on their own.

Leaving Comments

If you run into a blog entry or news story to which you want to add a comment, I encourage you to add your URL in the response. Do not make a blatant advertisement, but if you can leave your website address, do so. You never know who will read your comment and agree with you. That person might then take the time to visit your site. Just remember that your comment should be relevant to the news story or blog entry, not just an excuse to promote yourself.

Submitting Your Site to Web Directories

You might find lists or directories of sites that share your website's content. If you can find these sites (see Figure 17.2), find out how to get your site listed there by communicating with the people who run the list.

FIGURE 17.2
AYs Knitting blog list.

Using Social Media Power

Social media involves people sharing information with others whom they find important. Several sites, such as Digg.com, Reddit.com, and Stumbleupon.com, work in this manner. Explore these sites to find links to sites you might be interested in, and use them to promote your own sites.

You might have noticed a number of symbols appearing at the bottom of news stories or blog entries (see Figure 17.3). These symbols are links that allow the reader to share your article or blog post with others on social sharing websites such as Digg.com, Facebook.com, Delicious.com, and others. If you add these to your posts and someone clicks them, your content is shared with millions of other social media users. This goes both ways: If you find something you like, make sure to share it with others.

FIGURE 17.3
An example of website sharing.

Sites such as Twitter, MySpace, and Facebook also give you a canvass to promote your website. For example, you could use any of these sites to let people on your friends list know that you have new content on your website. For instance, on Facebook you can create notes to promote websites. Why not promote your own?

Search Engines

Finally, you want to ensure that search engines are listing and finding your website correctly. This topic is covered in the next section of this chapter.

How Search Engines Work

You probably use a search engine every time you're on the Internet. A search engine is simply a way for you to find what you are looking for on the Internet. If you are looking for collectible typewriter ribbon tins, you go to a search engine such as Google.com and type in `collectible typewriter ribbon tins`. The search engine displays a list of relevant search results, with the most relevant pages appearing at the top of the list (see Figure 17.4). These are the links most people click on first. For this reason, you want your web page to appear as high as possible in the list.

FIGURE 17.4

You want your website listed high in the Google rankings.

To better understand how to prepare your website for getting the most out of search engines, you need to know how search engines work:

1. You add your website to the Internet. At first, when your site has been added, no search engine knows your site even exists.

2. A spider finds your page. Search engines use robotic programs called spiders. These spiders crawl the Internet following every link, gathering information about every page they find, and then reporting back to the search engine about the contents. Spiders also count the frequency of words used on your page to get some idea of what your page is about.

3. Search engines compile the information. The search engine then compiles all the information from all the spiders and determines how to rank the pages based on their individual logic. Each search engine is a little bit different.

4. A visitor institutes a search and finds your page. When people use a search engine and type in words that match the ones found on your website, they find your website.

If you go to a search engine and look for your website, what do you find? If you type in your URL, more than likely your website will come up high in the list (you hope at the top), but people might not know the URL of your site. You need to give them a way to find your site based on keywords.

Optimizing Your Site for Search Engines

Just because your site is listed on a website doesn't mean you will get millions of hits. Your website might be listed but far down on the list of websites. Search engine optimization helps your website move up the list. The following sections discuss some search optimization techniques.

Keywords

Keywords are simply words or phrases that describe your website and appear on it. For example, if your website is about knitting, there may be many words you use regularly on the site, such as needles, gauge, or yarn. These are the words that search engines use to catalog your site.

Meta Tags

The search engine spider crawls your website and finds most of the words that represent your website. You can add words in Hypertext Markup Language (HTML) in a meta tag that is specifically catalogued by web spiders (see Figure 17.5). Remember, this is an aid to the search engine, not a guaranteed top ranking on a results page. The following are HTML meta tags:

- **Description**—This tag enables you to write a description in your own words that some web crawlers catalogue. This gives you some control over what appears as a description in the page rankings.

- **Keywords**—This tag enables you to specify keywords you want to emphasize that might not appear in your page.

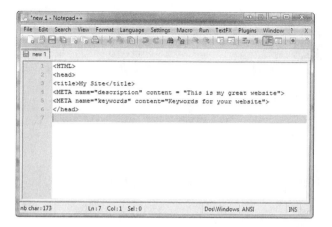

FIGURE 17.5

Using meta tags in HTML code.

17

To add a meta tag to your page, follow these steps:

1. Open your web page in your HTML editor.

2. In the `<head>` tag, insert a new line.

3. Type the following:

```
<META name="description" content ="The description of your
website">

<META name="keywords" content="Keywords for your website">
```

CAUTION

Although you want to increase your web traffic, don't try to "game the system" by adding search terms you think will be popular. It is considered bad form, and if people come to your site expecting one thing and find something else, they probably won't return. Focusing your description and keywords on what your site is really about will make it easier to find and more enjoyable for your visitors.

Maintaining Your Website

What? I'm Not Done?

A website is never finished. Think of it as a garden that needs constant attention. Maintaining your website gives you opportunities to make it a more fun and interesting place for your visitors. You need to perform a couple of key tasks regularly, the same way you would weed your garden and check your plants for bugs on a regular basis.

Unlike a garden, though, this process never stops when winter comes. You never really finish a website. The web is littered with sites that no one has kept up. Don't let your website become Internet litter.

Regular Maintenance

Maintenance on your website involves certain tasks to perform weekly, monthly, and annually. Try to set up a regular schedule so that you don't forget an important task. I make notes in my calendar for even the most mundane tasks so I don't forget.

Weekly Tasks

Try to get to these tasks once a week. Pick a time and day and just do it. Make it part of your schedule.

- **Check email links**—Make sure all email links work and you receive the email that the links send.
- **Test forms**—Test your forms to make sure the correct data is being logged and the correct information is being reported back to the visitor.

Monthly Tasks

Try to do these maintenance tasks at least once a month. Pick a day each month and stick to it.

- **Validate links**—Go through all your links at least once a month, either manually or using a link checker. Pay particular attention to external links, because they may change or go offline.
- **Check search engine ranking**—You should also occasionally check your place in search engines based on your keywords.

Annual Tasks

- **Renew domain name**—You must renew your domain name once a year. Your hosting service typically reminds you to do this simple task.
- **Check browsers**—New browsers and new versions come out all the time. I generally test my sites when a new version comes out, but if you do the browser testing once a year, you should be okay.
- **Back up files**—Even if you have made no major changes to your site in a year, you should still back up your files. You can never have enough backups, but you have to do it at least once a year.
- **Review your SSL certification**—If you are using Secure Sockets Layer (SSL) security on your site, you might need to renew your certificate annually.

The Power of Analytics

A common question people have about their websites is, "How do I track how many people come to my site?" This is not an easy question to answer. If your mom comes to your website 15 times in one day, does that count as 1 visitor or 15? Also, if you can get information about how many visitors you have, what other information can you get?

This information is commonly called analytics. Web developers can use this information to see how their website is being used and change and maintain it accordingly.

Most servers have a default level of data capture and data collection that is automatic. This means that every time a visitor comes to that web server, the web server captures some data about that visitor. This data goes beyond just counting who visited the site. It contains information such as when different people visited, what sites led them to your site, which browsers they were using, and what their operating systems were.

Common Analytics and What They Mean

Analytics provide statistics that can help you make decisions about improving your website. There are some excellent analytics programs out there that can help you see all the data about your website and enable you to capture more of it.

Most web servers track this sort of data, but you might not have access to your server. Ask your provider whether you can access analytical data. If this isn't possible, you might want to try a free service such as Google Analytics, which is discussed later in this chapter. Here is a list of the most common analytics that web servers gather and what they mean:

- **Hits**—These are individual files your web server sends to a visitor's browser. This means if you have a web page with six images on it, a visitor who comes to the site registers six hits. If the same visitor refreshes the page, six more hits are logged. This inflation is why hits are not a reliable tool for measuring how many people come to your site.

- **Page views**—This stat is the number of pages downloaded, no matter how many files comprise that page. So a visitor who comes to a page counts as one, and if that visitor refreshes the page, another page view is logged.

18

■ **Unique visitors**—This is the number of individual Internet Protocol (IP) addresses that access your site. This is more representative of the number of visitors, but if many people use the same computer at a school or library, the numbers might be incorrect.

■ **Downloads**—This is a count of files downloaded from your site that you want downloaded. For example, if you have a PDF of a form, this number tells you how many times visitors have downloaded it.

■ **Entry pages**—These are the pages on which people enter your website. Most of the time you want people to come to your home page, but sometimes someone links to a particular page on your website. This tells you what people come to your website hoping to find.

■ **Exit pages**—These are the pages from which people leave your website. It is easy to guess why they leave, but it could really be anything. For example, a page of links to other sites might be a place from which a large number of people leave your site.

■ **Referrers**—These are websites that have links to your site on which people have clicked to arrive on your site. Keep an eye on these to see whether new people are referencing you, and look at what they are saying. If they recommend your site for something, drop them a line thanking them.

■ **Search strings**—These are search terms that people use to find your site. They help you ensure that search engines are finding you correctly.

■ **Avg. time on site**—This is the average time a person has been on your site from entry to exit. Don't be upset if this is a low number; you are not on most websites all that long, either.

■ **New visitors**—These are the visitors who come to your website for the first time.

■ **Browsers used**—This tells you what browsers and versions visitors use. This helps you know what browsers to check when testing your website with different browsers.

Using Google Analytics

The best of the analytic sites is Google Analytics. All you need to do is register your website with Google Analytics, add some code to your website, and then go to the Google Analytics site to see who has been visiting your site.

Google Analytics gives you a ton of data—almost anything you would want to know about the people visiting your site. Here are some of the highlights:

- Number of visits
- Page views
- Pages per visit
- Average time on site
- Percent of new visits

Google Analytics also offers a number of statistics based on traffic sources and content.

Starting Google Analytics

If you don't have a Google account, the instructions for creating one appear in Chapter 9, "Web Page Services." If you do have a Google account, log in to it.

1. Go to www.google.com/analytics/. Google Analytics (see Figure 18.1) allows you access to your site's analytics.

FIGURE 18.1

The Google Analytics website.

2. Click the Access Analytics button.

3. After you access Google Analytics for the first time, you are asked to sign up for the service (see Figure 18.2).

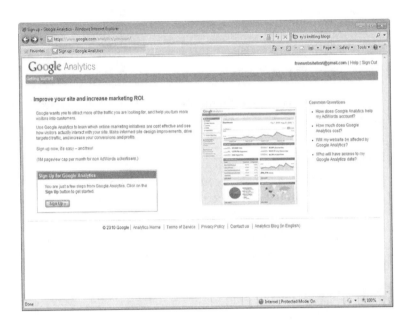

FIGURE 18.2
The sign-up page for Google Analytics.

Setting Up a New Account

After you have logged in to Google Analytics, follow these steps to set up a new account (see Figure 18.3):

1. Choose the website you want to track with Google Analytics.

2. Enter the website's uniform resource locator (URL).

3. Enter a name to be displayed when you look at the analytics for the website.

4. Select a time zone country and time zone from the drop-down list.

5. Click Continue.

6. Enter your first and last name in the name boxes, and the phone number if you wish.

7. Select your country from the drop-down list.

8. Click Continue.

9. Read the Google Analytics Terms of Service.

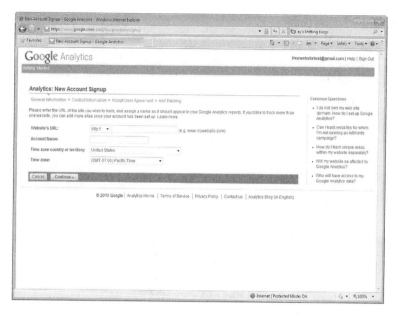

FIGURE 18.3

Sign up for a new account on this page.

10. Click the Yes box.
11. Click Create New Account.
12. The tracking code is then displayed (see Figure 18.4).

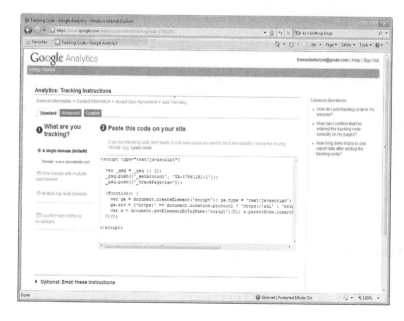

FIGURE 18.4

This tracking code is how Google Analytics monitors your website.

Applying the Tracking Code

The tracking code is JavaScript code, and you need to add it to every page you want to track, before the </body> tag.

tip If you use a website, such as a blog, with a footer file, you need to put the tracking code in only that one file to have it linked to every page.

1. Copy the script from the Tracking Code box.

2. Paste this code into every page you want tracked.

After you have added the code to your site, return to the analytics page. Your Analytics Settings now displays the page you are tracking and the status of information gathering (see Figure 18.5).

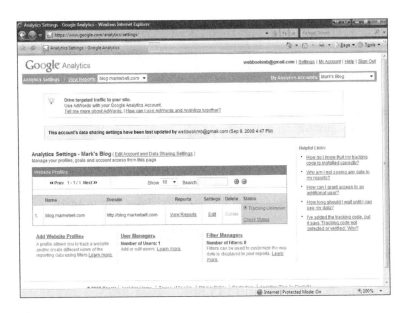

FIGURE 18.5
Google Analytics takes a few hours to begin collecting data.

Viewing Reports

After you have added your site to Google Analytics, you must give it some time to gather data. I know you are going to want to see results immediately, but Google Analytics monitors thousands of sites, so it takes a few hours for the data to trickle in. Here's how you can view your Google Analytics report:

1. Log in to Google Analytics.
2. Click the View Reports link.

The basic report for the website is displayed (see Figure 18.6).

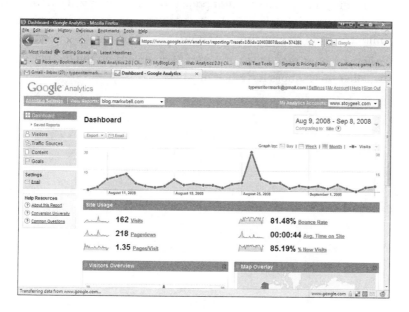

FIGURE 18.6

The basic Google Analytics report.

This is just the beginning of using Google Analytics. Have a look around, and check out all the statistics available.

Other Analytics Sites

There are other analytics sites on the Internet, but most of them offer only a simple set of features, with additional features for a fee. Here are some examples:

- Piwik—http://piwik.org/
- Clicky Web Analytics—www.getclicky.com/
- MyBlogLog—www.mybloglog.com/

Tweaking Your Site Based on Analytics

After you have captured a number of analytics, you will want to look at them and decide how to change your website. For example, if you have a lot of traffic to one page, make sure that page is at the front of your website. Also, if you are getting visitors who don't go to other pages on your website, you might want to change things around.

After you have made these changes, keep an eye on the analytics to see whether the changes have had an effect.

18

Building a Blog Using WordPress

Blogging is something you might have heard about over the past few years. What began as personal journals online has expanded to change the way journalism, politics, and businesses are communicating. This project covers what a blog is and how to use open-source software called WordPress to build your own blog. WordPress runs on a website that allows you to create blogs hosted by WordPress. Also, to run and manage your own blog, you can download the WordPress software and install it on your own web host.

What Is a Blog?

A blog is simply a web journal or log. The word *blog* is just a shortened form of *web log*. People have been writing logs and diaries for as long as there has been writing. Blogging is an electronic extension of these written words.

To put it simply, a blog is a list of dated entries that have the latest entry at the top of the web page.

The subject matter can be anything—and I do mean anything. There are blogs about food, knitting, politics, and anything that gives you the urge to write. I write a blog, my wife writes a blog, and her mother writes three blogs. (I always knew my mother-law had a lot of things to say, and now so does everyone else.) You can write about anything. The best advice is to write about something you love. You don't even have to be an expert.

Why Should I Blog?

When you tell some folks that you write a blog or ask them about blogging, they can't imagine why anyone would want to write a blog. They comment, "I have nothing to say," or "Who would be interested in what I have to say?" To be honest, I think everyone has something to say, and who cares if only one other person reads your blog?

Actually, you would be surprised who does listen to you. Blogging is a cheap and easy way to share your thoughts on anything you are interested in.

Blog Publishing

One of the web's innovations is the ease of publishing things such as blogs. Before the Internet, you had to have a printing press or convince a publisher to print something you had written. The Internet cuts out the middle man and enables anyone to publish easily. When blogging began, a blog was just a web page. The page had to be created in HTML and was a serious amount of work. So to add a new blog entry, the early blogger needed to write Hypertext Markup Language (HTML) code. This was a hassle, to say the least. Over time, websites specifically meant for bloggers began to show up. One of these was LiveJournal.com. LiveJournal made writing a blog easy. You signed up for an account and were off blogging about whatever you wanted to in no time flat. The problem was that, for some people, LiveJournal was too restrictive. Bloggers could not create their live journals exactly the way they envisioned them. People wanted more control.

19

Syndication

Ever have the feeling you are missing something that's happening, maybe something on the web? It could be a stock tip, a big news story, or good news about your Aunt Winona. Syndication helps with that. With blogs and other sites, but predominantly with blogs, syndication enables you to have that website alert you when something's been updated.

What Is WordPress?

WordPress is a company offering two services that are run out of two websites: WordPress.com and WordPress.org. WordPress.com enables you to set up and create blogs on their website. WordPress.org (run by the same folks) enables you to download the WordPress software and set it up on your own hosting site. If you are new in the blogging world, try starting with WordPress.com.

WordPress.com is one of the biggest blog sites in the world. It hosts more than 3 million blogs and hundreds of thousands of posts. The site serves as a hosting site and a home for the open-source version of the WordPress software. Not only can you set up a blog in just a few minutes, you can search for other blogs and communicate with other users who use WordPress.com. Using WordPress.com is 100% free.

If you are up for something a little more difficult and you want a little more freedom, learn how to install WordPress software on your own web host, which is covered in the second part of this chapter.

Software Versions

Like most software, WordPress has a version. A version number is a simple way for people using and developing the software to ensure they are using and talking about the same thing. For this chapter, I will be talking about WordPress version 2.6. You will probably be working with a later version, so there might be slight changes to the way the software works. As a rule of thumb, you should have the latest version of the software.

Five Reasons to Use WordPress.com to Host Your Blog

- **You are brand new to blogging**—WordPress.com makes it easy to get up and running quickly while connecting you to a larger community of more experienced bloggers.

19

■ **You have low technical ability**—WordPress.com is a nice and easy way to take advantage of some complicated technology in a way that you never have to worry about.

■ **You don't want to spend money for a blog**—A Wordpress.com blog is free. You can't save more money than that!

■ **You don't care about bells and whistles**—If you want a simple, well-run, robust blog and don't care about the latest gadgets or add-ins, WordPress.com is for you.

■ **You don't need your own domain**—All WordPress.com blogs are hosted under the WordPress.com domain. If not having your own domain isn't an issue for you, WordPress.com might be a good choice for you.

Five Reasons to Create Your Blog Using WordPress Software

■ **You have your own domain**—If you want a specific domain name, no problem. The WordPress software has no domain name restrictions.

■ **You want a different theme than the default**—You can find thousands of WordPress themes all over the Internet. Running your own version of WordPress software enables you to use them.

■ **You care about bells and whistles**—If you want all the add-ons and the ability to control every detail of your WordPress blog, you might want to download the software.

■ **You have good technical knowledge**—Installing, configuring, and using WordPress software requires knowledge of some technical things.

■ **Your hosting service offers WordPress installs**—My hosting service lets me automatically install WordPress. This gives me the best of both worlds.

Building a Blog Using WordPress.com

Let's imagine how someone might use a blog. Bill is a woodworker who loves the smell of sawdust in his workshop. He goes to the lumberyard and picks out his supplies, takes them home, and makes cabinets for his wife to put the family china in. He is proud of his work and enjoys the compliments visitors to his home pay him. One day, Bill heard from a friend that there were woodworking blogs on the Internet. In the past, Bill used the Internet only to look up an address or movie times; he never thought of looking for information about woodworking. At home, he began looking into his passion for wood and found hundreds of woodworking blogs. People had written blog entries on plans, wood shop design, choosing materials, and all things related to woodworking.

Bill loved reading about other people doing woodworking projects. He also loved looking at pictures taken both during construction and upon completion. After reading a number of blogs, Bill decided he wanted to try it on his own. Let's build Bill his own woodworking blog.

This section of the chapter covers getting a blog up and running on WordPress.com. If you are interested in running your own version of WordPress and hosting it somewhere else, you should skip ahead to the "Setting Up Your Own Blog with WordPress Software" section of this chapter.

Before you begin at WordPress.com, you need the following:

- An idea for your blog
- A name for your blog
- An email address

Signing Up for WordPress.com

Before you begin using WordPress.com, you need to sign up for the service. Don't worry—it's free and gives you access to WordPress.com software and a whole community of people using it.

> **caution** Because WordPress.com is a website that is constantly being updated, these instructions may be different from what you see.

1. Open your web browser and navigate to www.WordPress.com. This is the home page for WordPress.com, and it's where you sign up for blog hosting service (see Figure 19.1).

2. Click the Sign Up Now button. The Sign Up page appears (see Figure 19.2). On this page, enter all the information you need to set up your blog on the WordPress.com servers.

3. In the Username field, enter a username for your WordPress.com account. When choosing a username, you want to make it unique and easy for you to remember. For example, Bill might choose something like "woodworkingbill." WordPress.com requires your username to be at least four characters long and have only lowercase letters and numbers in it.

19

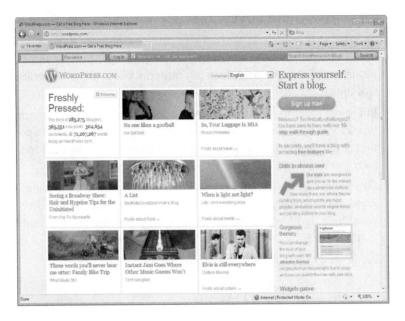

FIGURE 19.1
The WordPress.com front page.

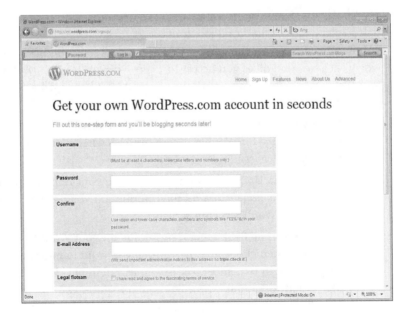

FIGURE 19.2
The Sign Up page for WordPress.com.

4. Next, in the Password field, enter a word or phrase you are going to use for your password. As you enter your password, WordPress.com evaluates whether it is a good one. When choosing a password, make it unique and easy to remember. Try to have a combination of letters and numbers. The case of the letters matters also, so use a combination of upper- and lowercase. WordPress.com also allows you to use the characters !"£$%^&(in your password.

5. In the Confirm field, enter your password again. WordPress.com asks you to confirm your password to make sure you entered the same password both times.

6. In the Email Address field, enter your email address. This enables WordPress.com to communicate information and administration notes. Make sure it is correct.

7. Beside the Legal Flotsam box, click Fascinating Terms of Service. This opens the Terms of Service page (see Figure 19.3). Terms of Service is a nice title for a bunch of legal information about using the WordPress.com website. You should read over this if you have the time and patience.

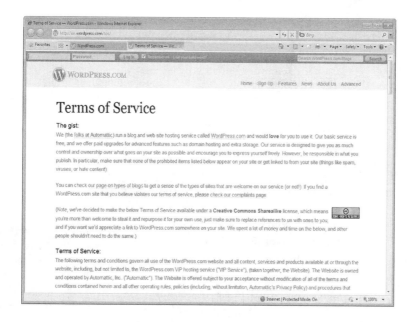

FIGURE 19.3

Only a lawyer would find the Terms of Service page interesting.

8. When you are finished with the Terms of Service page, click the Back button on your browser. You are returned to the WordPress.com Sign Up page.

9. When you return to the Sign Up page, the Legal Flotsam box should be checked. If it isn't, check it now.

10. Next, because you are here to create a blog, click the Gimme a Blog button.

11. Click Next. This opens the Blog Information page (see Figure 19.4). You use this page to give basic information about the blog you are starting.

FIGURE 19.4

This is information about your blog on WordPress.com.

12. The Blog Domain field is filled out with what WordPress.com thinks you might want as your blog domain address. This is a *subdomain* of the WordPress.com domain, so you don't need to pay domain fees or register it. You can edit the Blog Domain only once, so choose wisely. You can use letters and numbers only (no symbols), and you need to have at least four characters.

caution After you click Signup at the bottom of the page, you cannot change the blog domain. Double-check it before proceeding.

13. The Blog Title field is filled out with what WordPress.com thinks you might want as your blog title address. You can change this at any time. Make the name representative of what you want to talk about in the blog. Bill chooses Bill's Wood Working Weblog.

14. Select the language you want your blog and configuration pages to use. Your blog comes with several things: navigation, configuration, and help pages that are displayed in a particular language.

15. Select your privacy settings. If you want your blog to be listed in search engines such as Google and Technorati and in public listings around WordPress.com, click the check box beside Privacy. If you prefer to keep your blog more private, ensure that this Privacy box is unchecked.

16. Click Signup. You are now signed up with WordPress.com with your very own blog. Next, you need to activate your account.

> ## 🎙 Geek Speak
>
> **subdomain**
>
> A subdomain is a domain under an existing domain. Typing `blog1.domain.com` or `blog2.domain.com` leads to the same domain and different sub-domains. A domain can have unlimited subdomains under it.

Activating Your Account

After you have signed up for WordPress.com, you need to activate your account. WordPress.com is a public website that bad guys can use for bad things. These bad guys want to use WordPress.com's servers for nefarious purposes. To keep bad behavior to a minimum, WordPress.com asks you to activate your account.

WordPress.com sends an email to the address you provided when you signed up. The website tells you it can take up to half an hour to get the email, but it is usually instantaneous. When you receive the email message, read it and follow the instructions in the email. The instructions include a link to activate your blog.

After you have clicked on the link to activate your blog, WordPress.com tells you that your site is active and gives you your username and password. Now you're ready to log in to your blog or view it (see Figure 19.5).

Notice that a blog entry is here already. WordPress.com creates a blog entry so you can see what one looks like. The title of the entry is "Hello World," and the text welcomes you to blogging with WordPress.com.

FIGURE 19.5
This is your blog!

Logging In to Your Blog

When you have a blog on WordPress.com, you have a public side and a behind-the-scenes side. The public side is what the world sees when they visit your blog domain. WordPress.com calls the behind-the-scenes side the Dashboard. It's where you write and manage entries, change the look of the blog, and do other administrative tasks. When you log in to your blog, you are given access to the Dashboard. You can log in to your WordPress.com blog in the following ways:

- Go to http://USERNAME.wordpress.com/wp-login.php.

- On your blog, choose Login under the *Meta menu*.

- Go to WordPress.com and sign in under Already Hip. Then select your blog under Your Blogs.

Logging in to WordPress.com by any of these methods brings you to the same place—your WordPress.com Dashboard (see Figure 19.6).

Geek Speak

Meta menu

The Meta menu is the menu on your blog that lets you access admin pages. It is nothing more than links to special pages.

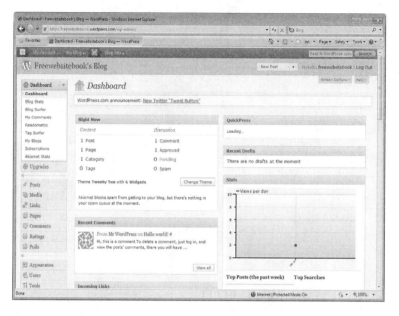

FIGURE 19.6

This is your blog's Dashboard.

The WordPress.com Dashboard is a set of pages that enable you to do the following:

- Write blog posts
- Manage blog posts
- Change the design of your blog
- Manage the comments on your blog

The next section of this project covers all these activities.

Writing Blog Posts

Now that you have created your blog, what's next? Well, you need to fill it with blog entries! You do this by writing a new blog entry.

1. On the Dashboard, click the New Post button at the top of the page. This opens the Write Post screen. This is the page you use to add new posts to your blog (see Figure 19.7). Posting a blog entry has two steps:

   1. **Saving**—When you save the post, it is stored in your blog.

   2. **Publishing**—When you publish a blog post, it becomes visible to people looking at your blog.

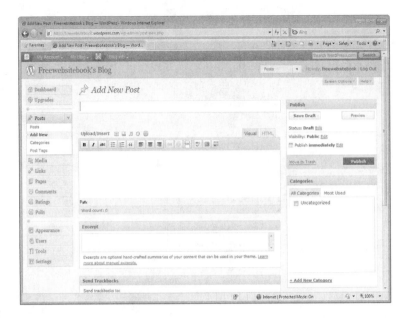

FIGURE 19.7

This is where you write your blog entries.

2. Enter a title for your blog post in the Title field. The title appears at the top of the blog entry and acts as a hyperlink to it. Your blog can be viewed as all your entries or one entry at a time. When you click on the blog entry title, only that entry is displayed.

3. Enter the blog post in the Post field, which is a special kind of text box. When you type in the box, the text looks as it will appear on the blog. This is sometimes called WYSIWYG (what you see is what you get).

   You can bold, italicize, and make text appear with a strike through it. There are a number of other formatting options for the text, including margins, bullets, and automatic numbering. This is the meat of your blog entry. Experiment with this part of writing blogs, and add pictures or other multimedia elements if they seem appropriate. Look at other blogs, see what they include, and if you like a feature, add it to your blog.

Geek Speak

WYSIWYG

WYSIWYG stands for what you see is what you get. It is pronounced *whizzy-wig*, and it means the text and graphics appear when you create them as they will in the finished document.

4. After you have edited your post, click Save. The post is now saved to your blog.

5. When you are ready for other people to see your post, click Publish. Now your blog post is visible to anyone who goes to your blog. Don't worry: If you want to, you can unpublish the post.

6. Go to your blog and check out your new entry.

Managing Blog Posts

After you have some blog entries created, you might need to manage them. The management functions include

■ Seeing the current status of posts

■ Editing existing entries

■ Viewing stats of posts

On the Dashboard, click the Manage tab near the top of the page. This opens the Manage Posts screen (see Figure 19.8). This is the page you use to manage posts to your blog. It lists all the posts currently saved on the blog, with the most recent post at the top of the list. It also shows you who wrote the post and what its current status is.

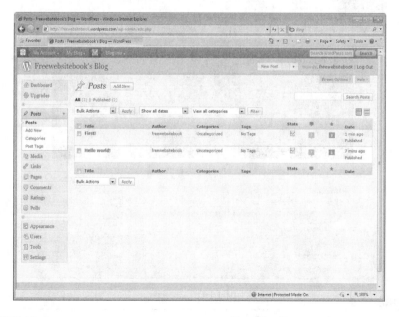

FIGURE 19.8

This is the page you use to manage blog entries.

■ To edit a blog post, click Title or Edit.

■ To view the stats of a post, click the status icon on the end of each post's entry.

■ To search the posts, enter what you are looking for in the Search field and click Search Posts.

Changing the Design of Your Blog

The design of your blog is how it appears to your blog viewers. WordPress.com has templates of designs called themes.

When you sign up for your blog, you can choose from among a number of preloaded themes that cover a range of looks and features. Again, have fun exploring different looks for your blog.

Here's how to change the theme of your web log:

1. On the Dashboard, click Appearance on the left side.

2. Select a theme and click on it. You can also preview or activate a theme by clicking the links below the thumbnail image. A preview of the theme applied to your blog appears (see Figure 19.9).

FIGURE 19.9

The blog with a theme choice displayed.

3. To apply the theme to your blog, click Activate in the top-right corner. To go back to your original design, click the X (Close icon) in the left corner.

Keep checking your Design page, because new designs are sometimes added, and something new may be more to your liking.

Manage the Comments on Your Blog

People who read your blog may have something to say about your posts. A comment is a textual addition to a blog entry. If people read your post and feel compelled to leave a reply, WordPress.com gives them an easy way to do this. WordPress.com also enables you to moderate the comments. That means you can decide what comments are visible on your blog.

With WordPress.com, you can approve, mark as *spam*, unapprove, or delete comments.

On the Dashboard, click the Manage tab near the top of the page. This opens the Manage Comments screen, which is where you can manage comments on your blog.

Geek Speak

spam

Just like your email box, your blog can have spam comments added to it. The term spam refers to unwanted solicitations to your email or blog. Lots of people will try to fill your blog with spam comments, but WordPress.com helps you keep this to a minimum.

- To approve a comment, hover over the listing and click Approve. This makes it visible to anyone reading your blog.

- If you find a spam comment, select the check box beside it and click Mark as Spam. This reports the origin of the comment to WordPress.com as spam in an effort to lower the number of spam comments on everyone's blogs.

- To remove a comment you previously approved, select the check box beside it and click Unapprove. This makes the comment invisible to anyone reading your blog.

- To permanently delete a comment, select the check box beside it and click Delete. This removes the comment from your blog.

19

Setting Up Your Own Blog with WordPress Software

What if you've already tried the WordPress.com solution and been happy with it, but you want to expand the functions of your blog or enhance the look and feel? Or maybe you're more of a techie geek and you want something more than WordPress.com has to offer. If so, here's the "wait, there's more" that you've been expecting.

If you want to have more control over your blog site and have the technical knowledge to install, configure, and maintain it, downloading the WordPress software from WordPress.org could be the solution for you. Setting up your blog with the WordPress software enables you to add your own plug-ins, design your own themes, and control when your software is updated.

Information You Need Before You Begin

Before you install your own WordPress software, you need to do a few things, such as backing up your files.

How WordPress Software Works

As you can imagine, quite a bit is going on in the background of WordPress software. It's important to know what parts are involved and how they work with each other. There are a number of parts working together to make your blog work correctly. When you use WordPress.com (as in the previous part of the chapter), all this is taken care of for you. When you use the WordPress software, you are on your own, so you need to understand the *architecture* of a WordPress blog (see Figure 19.10).

> **caution** When installing software on your own, you are venturing into new, uncharted territory. Things might not work as expected. Before beginning this process, back up anything important. And don't worry! It is difficult to break things during an install. Have fun with the process.

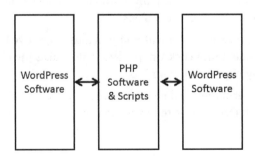

FIGURE 19.10

The architecture of a WordPress blog.

WordPress Software

This is the software that creates and runs your blog, including the website pages, themes, and add-ons.

PHP Software and Scripts

PHP is a scripting language that helps you create a dynamic web page using the WordPress software. The PHP scripts also talk to the MySQL database to gather data and build dynamic pages.

MySQL Database

This database houses all the information that makes up your blog. All the entries and configuration settings are stored in this database. For the most part, you don't need to know how this works, but it is good to know where the information part of your blog is stored.

Geek Speak

architecture

When you first hear the term architecture, you probably think of people sitting behind art tables designing buildings. What I mean in this instance is computer architecture. Architecture is just a fancy term for the relationship between different software and hardware. The architecture of a system describes what computers are involved and what software runs on them. It also describes how the data is transferred between these computers.

How Much Does All This Cost?

You are probably wondering how much this is going to cost you. Nothing. All the software you need to run WordPress is free. It isn't trial software that you use for only a period before you have to pay for it. This software is given away free. Do something amazing with it.

Before Installing Your Software

Before starting your installation of WordPress software, you need to do some simple things with your hosting service and get a few tools.

If you need help finding a host, see Chapter 2, "Choosing a Location for Your Site."

Confirm That the Right Software Is Installed on Your Server

To run WordPress 2.6, your web hosting service must provide the following:

- PHP version 4.3 or greater
- MySQL version 4.0 or greater

19

■ (Optional) Apache `mod_rewrite` module (for clean uniform resource indicators [URIs] known as Permalinks)

Get a Text Editor

You might have to edit some text files to get your WordPress install up and running. A text file is simply a file with words and numbers in it that doesn't contain formatting.

TextWrangler is an excellent Mac text editor. You can find it at www.barebones.com/products/textwrangler/index.shtml.

Get an FTP Client

FTP stands for File Transfer Protocol and is a fancy name for the software that allows you to easily transfer files between computers. When you are installing software such as WordPress, you need to move files between computers easily. An FTP client is a program that helps you do this.

Pick a Username and Password

A good rule of thumb is to pick a username and password before you begin. Make sure they're unique and contain letters and numbers.

Download and Install WordPress

This section covers how to download and install the open-source software from WordPress.org. Read the instructions carefully, and remember to back up any important files.

Download WordPress Software

The first step of setting up your own WordPress software is downloading it. Follow these steps to download the WordPress software:

1. Go to http://wordpress.org/download/.

2. Click the Download WordPress 3.0.1 button. A *zip file* is downloaded to your computer.

3. After the download completes, double-click the zip file to open it.

4. Unzip this file to your hard drive.

For the next steps, you need to consult WordPress documentation. Differences in hosts and how you install and configure WordPress affect what actions you should take. Here are some documentation sources to help you with your installation:

■ **Installing WordPress—** http://codex.wordpress. org/Installing_WordPress

■ **Installing WordPress on Tiger—** http://maczealots.com/tutorials/wordpress/

■ **Installing WordPress locally on Fedora Linux—** http://techiecat. catsgarden.net/archives/3

■ **Installing WordPress on Ubuntu with LAMP—** www.supriyadisw. net/2006/12/wordpress-installation-on-ubuntu-with-lamp

This is by no means a quick and easy process. Take your time, and read the instructions thoroughly.

Customization of WordPress

There are a lot of ways to customize your WordPress blog. The two main ways are to add new themes and plug-ins. Themes change the way your blog looks, and plug-ins add functionality.

Adding Themes

Many people are making themes beyond what comes installed with the WordPress software. A theme is just a collection of text and graphics files that tells WordPress how to display your blog information. Adding new themes is easy, and they offer all sorts of exciting looks to your blog.

Several excellent sites offer WordPress themes. You can do a web search for "WordPress themes" or go to the following sites:

■ **WordPress.org Official Theme Directory—**http://wordpress.org/ extend/themes/

■ **Best Word Press Themes—**www.bestwpthemes.com/

■ **Kate's Theme Viewer—**http://themes.rock-kitty.net

To install new themes, follow these steps:

1. Download the theme zip file from one of the locations just listed.

2. Extract the zip file to your hard drive. The zip file expands to a folder. Keep this folder exactly as it is unzipped.

3. Open your FTP client and connect to your host server.

4. Navigate to the wp-content/themes directory.

5. Move the complete theme folder into the themes directory.

6. Select the theme as previously described in the section "Changing the Design of Your Blog."

caution Don't pay for themes. There are literally thousands of free excellent WordPress themes, so don't waste your money!

Adding Plug-Ins

The best way to add functionality is through plug-ins. A plug-in is a group of programming files that tell WordPress what new functionality to add. Plug-ins run within WordPress and enable you to expand the functions of your website. Maybe you want to add a calendar or connect to Facebook, Twitter, or other Web 2.0 sites through your blog.

Several excellent sites have WordPress plug-ins. You can do a web search for "WordPress plug-ins" or go to the following sites:

- **Official WordPress Plug-Ins Repository**—http://wordpress.org/extend/plugins

- **WordPress Plug-in Database**—http://wp-plugins.net/beta

To download new plug-ins, follow these steps:

1. Download the plug-in zip file from one of the locations just listed.

2. Extract the zip file to your hard drive. The zip file expands to a folder. Keep this folder exactly as it is unzipped.

3. Open your FTP client and connect to your host server.

4. Navigate to the wp-content/plugins directory.

caution Don't pay for plug-ins. There are literally thousands of free excellent WordPress plug-ins, so don't waste your money!

19

5. Move the complete plug-in folder into the themes directory.

6. Log in to the administrator interface of your blog.

7. Click Plug-Ins on the top right of the interface.

> **caution** Don't do this unless you are comfortable with HTML and PHP or else you can screw up your whole blog. Be sure, as always, to back up your files.

8. On your blog, access the Plug-In Management Panel in your Administration panels.

9. In the list, find the plug-in you just installed.

10. Click Activate.

Personalization of WordPress

After customizing your own WordPress sites, you might want to go even further. Excellent! Now you'll want to make your WordPress blog unique. Common personalizations are things like creating or modifying themes, creating plug-ins, or even writing blog entries from your iPhone. Remember to back up your blog before you do this. This means storing a safe working copy of your blog on another computer.

Modifying Themes

Just because you download a theme and install it doesn't mean you're stuck with it. If you have the technical skill, WordPress enables you to access the plug-in files from the administrative interface and edit them.

1. Log in to the administrator interface of your blog.

> **caution** Don't do this unless you are very comfortable with HTML and PHP.

2. Click Appearance on the left side of the page.

3. Click Editor on the left side under Appearance. The theme editor (see Figure 19.11) enables you to edit the files that make up the theme you are currently using.

4. Select a file on the right side under Theme Files.

> **note** These steps change the version of the theme on your server only. If you do something that you don't like or that makes your blog go ACK!, just download the theme again and overwrite the files on your server.

19

5. Edit the file in the text box.

6. Click Update File.

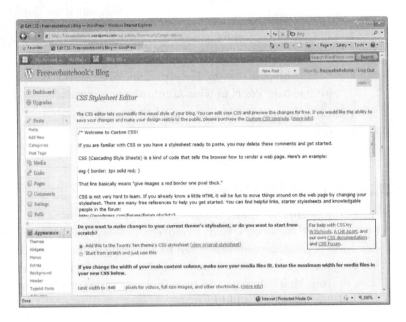

FIGURE 19.11
The theme editor enables you to edit your current theme.

Creating Themes

After working a bit with existing themes, you might want to create your own. Creating your own theme can help you customize the cascading style sheet (CSS), HTML/XHTML, and PHP to your personal needs.

The process of creating themes is covered on the following websites:

- **Theme Development**—http://codex.wordpress.org/Theme_Development

- **Templates**—http://codex.wordpress.org/Templates

- **Make Your Own WordPress Theme**— www.cypherhackz.net/archives/2006/12/13/make-your-own-wordpress-theme-part-1/

- **Anatomy of a WordPress Theme**—http://boren.nu/archives/2004/11/10/anatomy-of-a-wordpress-theme/

Creating Plug-Ins

Creating plug-ins is a more ambitious task. You really need to know how WordPress works inside and out before attempting this feat. Creating them takes quite a while and involves lots of testing and problem solving, but when a plug-in you have created works, it can be an awesome feeling of accomplishment.

Here are some plug-in creation resources:

- **Writing a Plugin**—http://codex.wordpress.org/Writing_a_Plugin
- **Plugin API**—http://codex.wordpress.org/Plugin_API
- **Your First WP Plugin (video)**—http://markjaquith.wordpress.com/ 2006/03/04/wp-tutorial-your-first-wp-plugin

Blogging on Your iPhone

One of the newest things you can do with WordPress is blog right from your iPhone. WordPress has an iPhone application that allows you to blog, add pictures, and preview your posts. You can even edit existing posts right from your iPhone. If you don't have an iPhone, just ignore this and let us lucky few tap on our screens.

1. Install the WordPress application from the Apple App Store.
2. Enter your blog information.
3. Blog on your iPhone. Just don't do it when you are driving!

For more information, see the WordPress iPhone page, http://iphone. wordpress.org/.

Keep an Eye on Things

WordPress is exciting blogging software that is always changing and improving. Keep a close eye on your blog and WordPress software announcements. Take part in the WordPress community, blog your heart out, and most importantly, have lots of fun!

Building a Business Site Using a Content Management System

A content management system (CMS) is an editable set of web pages that enables you to organize, categorize, and manage content through a web-based interface. So rather than build pages in HTML and then use an FTP client to move the files to a web server, you just log in to a web page and make content changes through your browser. A CMS can take many forms. For example, Facebook is a CMS that allows you to add, edit, and manage information about yourself through your web browser (see Figure 20.1). A CMS also allows multiple people to edit these pages.

In the first part of this chapter, you use a CMS (SocialGO) to set up your own social network. SocialGO lets you set up a social network in just a few minutes without having to mess with a web server. The second part of this chapter covers the open-source CMS, Joomla. Joomla is being used for business, education, and other industries. If you are unsure of whether to use SocialGO or Joomla, the following lists can help you decide which program is right for you.

FIGURE 20.1
Facebook.com is a CMS.

Five Reasons to Use SocialGO as Your CMS

- **You want to create a social network**—If you have a group of people with whom you want to connect in your own social network and want to have greater control over the look and content of the social network site than you would with Facebook or other social network sites, SocialGO is the place for you.

- **You are new to content management systems**—SocialGO makes it easy to get up and running quickly and connects you to a larger community of more experienced social network creators.

- **You have low technical ability**—SocialGO makes it easy to create your own full-featured social network.

- **You don't want to spend money for a CMS**—A basic SocialGO network is free. You can't save more money than that!

- **You don't need your own domain**—SocialGO's networks are hosted under the Socialgo.com domain, so there's no need to bother with creating and paying for your own domain.

Five Reasons to Use Joomla as Your CMS

■ **You want to create more than a social network**—SocialGO is a great tool for creating simple social networks, but Joomla has more robust features.

■ **You have your own domain**—If you want a specific domain name, the Joomla software has no domain name restrictions.

■ **You have some technical knowledge**—Installing, configuring, and using Joomla software requires some technical knowledge.

■ **You care about bells and whistles**—Joomla enables you to control every detail of your CMS.

■ **Your hosting service offers Joomla installs**—Some hosting services let you install Joomla automatically. This gives you more control and offers a simple installation.

What Is SocialGO?

SocialGO (see Figure 20.2) is a CMS that enables you to create your own social network, similar to Facebook.com. You can have your own social network to connect with friends, colleagues, family, or other like-minded people. SocialGO was launched in 2007 and has tried to fill the void left when ning.com became a pay site.

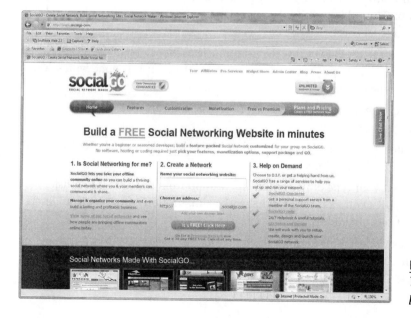

FIGURE 20.2
The SocialGO home page.

20

Building a Social Network with SocialGO

SocialGO offers a free version that displays some SocialGO promotional links and has 1GB of storage and 10GB of bandwidth. This is a great place to start. SocialGO makes it simple to get a social networking site up and running in no time.

Before you get started at SocialGO, you need the following:

- A name for your social network
- An address (URL, or uniform resource locator) for your social network
- An email address

caution Because SocialGO.com is a website that is constantly being updated, these instructions may be different from what you see.

Sign Up for SocialGO

Before you begin using SocialGO, you need to sign up for the service. The basic service is free and allows you access to the software and a whole community of people using SocialGO. This is how you sign up for SocialGO:

1. Open your web browser and navigate to www.socialgo.com. This opens the home page for SocialGO.com, where you sign up for the service.

2. Enter the name of your social network in the Create a Network box.

3. Enter the address for your social network in the Choose an Address box. This address needs to be six letters and can contain only numbers and letters.

4. Click the It's FREE! Click Here button. The Choose Your SocialGO Account Type page appears (see Figure 20.3). On this page, you select the type of account you want on SocialGO.com.

5. Click Continue at the bottom of the Free column. The network details page is displayed.

6. Enter the name of your network in the field. Add your address if one is not displayed already.

7. Select your type of network configuration from the drop-down list. SocialGO offers a range of network configurations that give you different sets of features.

8. Next, select your network design template. SocialGO offers a number of nice templates and features. Once you have a template selected, click the Continue button. This takes you to the Account Details screen.

FIGURE 20.3

The Ready to Start Your Free Trial? page.

9. In the Your Name field, enter your name.

10. In the Email Address and the Confirm Email Address fields, enter your email address. Giving your email address allows SocialGO to communicate information and administration notes. Make sure it is correct.

11. In the Password field, enter a word or phrase you are going to use for your password. When choosing a password, make it unique and easy to remember. Try to have a mixture of letters and numbers. The case of the letters matters also, so use a mixture of upper- and lowercase.

12. In the Confirm Password field, enter your password again.

13. Enter the code as it appears in the box to the right of the empty box. Click the Terms of Service box after reading the Terms of Service.

14. Click the Continue button. This opens your social network (see Figure 20.4). A video takes you through the steps to customizing your social network.

20

FIGURE 20.4
Your new social network.

Invite Friends

Now that you have a social network site, you need to invite some friends. Your friends will add content and take part in your social network. To invite your friends to your social network, follow these steps:

1. On the main page of your social network, click the Invite Contacts button. This opens the Contact Importer window (see Figure 20.5), where you can add your contacts from different email services to the friends that you want to join you on your social network or you can enter the email address of friends.

2. Enter the email addresses of your friends in the Email Address box. If there are multiple emails, use commas to separate them.

3. Click Invite Contacts. This sends out email invitations (which include instructions) to your social network.

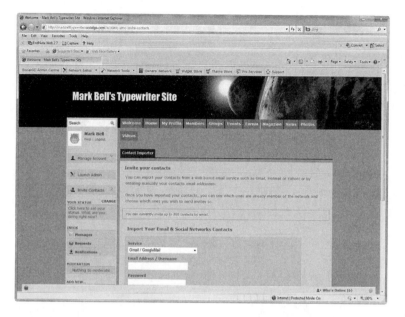

FIGURE 20.5
The Contact Importer window.

Add Photos and Video

You can add photos or videos to your social network to give your new members something to look at or watch. To add photos or videos, follow these two steps:

1. On the main page of your social network, click the Add Photos or Add a Video button. This opens the Add Photos window (see Figure 20.6) or the Add Video window.

2. Use the Browse button to locate a photo or video, and click Add. Your photos or videos are added to your social network.

20

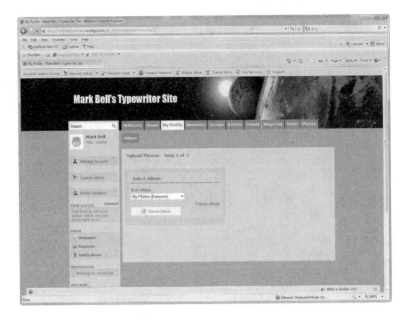

FIGURE 20.6

The Add Photos window.

Start Admin Center

An important part of a social network is the Admin Center. You use the Admin Center to configure your SocialGO.com social network.

1. On the main page of your social network, click the Launch Admin button. This opens the Admin Center page (see Figure 20.7).

2. Enter your credentials and log in. This opens the Admin Center (see Figure 20.8).

FIGURE 20.7
The Admin Center window.

FIGURE 20.8
The Admin Center page.

Building a Site with Joomla

Joomla is one of the best open-source CMS software programs available because it's easy to use and has some of the best features (see Figure 20.9). It's also free. Unlike SocialGO, Joomla gives you total control of the configuration of your site.

FIGURE 20.9

The Joomla home page.

Joomla can be used to run a social network, a blog, or even more complex information structures. It doesn't enforce a use like SocialGO does, so you can use the software for many types of sites.

Joomla also has a robust developer community that you can access to gain information about extending your Joomla installation or fixing problems you might have.

Before you install the Joomla software, you need to do a few things. Read on.

> **caution** When installing software on your own, there is a possibility that things will go wrong and might not work as expected. It's important to back up anything important before beginning this process, just in case.

20

Before Installing Your Joomla Software

Before starting your install of Joomla software, you need to do some simple things with your hosting service, and you need some tools.

1. Check to ensure that the right software is installed on your server. To run Joomla 1.5.x, your web hosting service must provide the following:

   ■ PHP version 5.0 or greater (5.1.x is recommended)

   ■ MySQL version 5.0 or greater

2. Get a text editor. You might have to edit some text files to get your Joomla install up and running. For more information about good text editors, refer to Chapter 5, "Gathering Your Tools."

   > **note** Without access to PHP and MySQL on your web server, you cannot run Joomla software. If one of these pieces is missing, you need to use SocialGO.com or look for another CMS solution.

3. Get an FTP client. When you are installing software such as Joomla, you need an FTP client to move files between machines. For more information about FTP clients, refer to Chapter 5.

4. Pick a username and password that are unique and contain letters and numbers.

Download and Install Joomla

To begin using Joomla, you need to download it and install the software on your web server. To download the Joomla software, go to http://joomlacode.org (see Figure 20.10). This is the main source for the Joomla code. You need to register before downloading the Joomla code.

Depending on your host, installing and configuring Joomla from this point might be tricky, so if you have any questions, consult the Joomla documentation. There is even an easy browser version of the installation you might be able to use depending on your server. Here are some documentation sources to help you with your installation.

   ■ **Joomla! 1.5 Installation Manual**—http://downloads.joomlacode.org/ docmanfileversion/1/7/4/17471/1.5_Installation_Manual_version_0.5. pdf

   ■ **Joomla Browser Installation**—http://help.joomla.org/content/view/ 39/132

20

▪ **How to Install Joomla!**—http://battractive.com/Joomla/Joomla-Install-small.pdf

FIGURE 20.10

The Joomla download page.

After you have downloaded and installed Joomla, you'll notice that its operation is similar to SocialGO. For example, you can add pages, content, and discussions like you did in SocialGO, but Joomla gives you advanced features such as user management, modules, plug-ins, and templates, and it places no limitations on size.

Like using WordPress software, there is a publicly viewable front part of the website and a password-protected area, where you administer your Joomla installation. In the administrative section of the website, you can add articles, manage users, and apply modules, plug-ins, and templates.

20

Adding Articles

Articles are like stories or posts you add to your Joomla website. When you add an article, it appears on the front page like a blog entry. Follow these instructions to add an article:

1. Point your browser to http://yourdomain.com/administrator/index. php?option=com_login.

2. Log in to Joomla! Administration with the credentials you gave during your Joomla installation. This opens the administrator area of your Joomla site (see Figure 20.11).

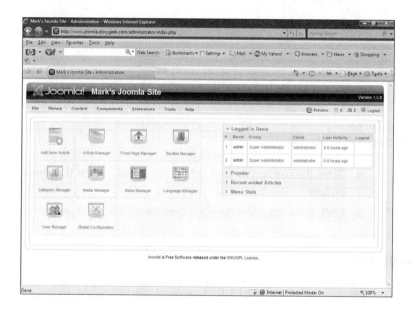

FIGURE 20.11

The Joomla Administrator page.

3. Click the Add New Article button. This opens the New Article editor (see Figure 20.12).

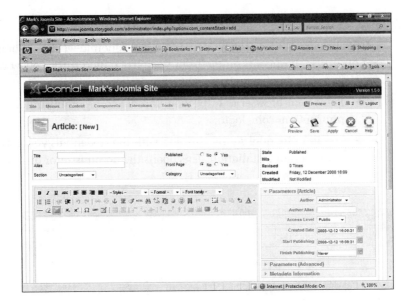

FIGURE 20.12
The Joomla New Article page.

4. Enter the content of your article, and click Yes on the Front Page radio button.

5. Click Save. Your article now appears on the front page.

Managing Users

Joomla has robust user management, which means you can add new users and give them specific abilities (such as creating, editing, and accessing certain parts of the website). You access the User Manager from the Administration interface (see Figure 20.13).

FIGURE 20.13
The Joomla User Manager.

Modules, Plug-Ins, and Templates

Modules, plug-ins, and templates are customizations you can add to your Joomla installation. They allow a range of features such as calendars, polls, image slide shows, and extensions to other websites. Here are some module, plug-in, and template resources:

- **Joomla Extensions (http://extensions.joomla.org)**—This site contains a great collection of modules and plug-ins for your Joomla site.

- **Joomla Hacks (www.joomlahacks.com)**—This is a techie resource for all things Joomla.

Here are a few additional Joomla resources:

- **What Is Joomla?**—www.joomla.org/about-joomla.html
- **Joomla Tutorials**—www.joomlatutorials.com
- **The Joomla! Community Portal**—http://community.joomla.org

20

Keep an Eye on Things

Joomla is a dynamic CMS software program that is always changing and improving. Keep a close eye on your Joomla software announcements, take part in the Joomla community, and have fun using the resources discussed in this chapter!

Building a Multimedia Website

Great websites require not only great content, but great multimedia. Whether you're showing multimedia demos of products for your company or music for your band, using multimedia is the best way to illustrate this content. For a great example of the use of multimedia, check out Blendtec, which uses multimedia and humor to increase its high-end blender sales (see Figure 21.1).

Chapter 12, "Working with Multimedia," covered how to prepare multimedia elements for use on your website. This project covers how to use some common types of multimedia files on a website: podcasts, audio files, video files, and Flash files. With the skills learned in this project, you'll be able to create a dynamic, vibrant website that looks as if you spent a fortune on it.

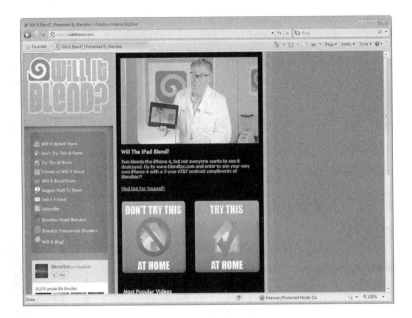

FIGURE 21.1
Will It Blend? is a popular multimedia site.

Best Practices for Multimedia

You should keep some best practices in mind as you build your multimedia website. These tips will help you avoid common mistakes that people make when using multimedia on their sites. If you've spent any time browsing the web, you've probably seen many sites that make some of these mistakes.

- **Do not make multimedia elements play automatically**—This is a big no-no. Don't you hate it when you visit a website and it immediately blares music or video at you, especially when you are at work? It is the equivalent of inviting someone into your house and then shouting at them when they arrive. Make playing a multimedia file the visitor's choice.

- **Meta tag your multimedia elements**—If you use meta tags with your multimedia (see Chapter 17, "Promoting Your Website"), search engines pick up your content.

- **Link to browser plug-in sites**—If your multimedia files use browser plug-ins to play, add a link to a site where people can download that plug-in.

- **If the file is large, warn people**—If any of your multimedia files are downloadable, warn people about the ones that are large. Better yet, tell them the size of the files. No one likes starting a download of a multimedia file only to find out it is going to take all night. You may want to add estimated download times.

- **Not every site needs multimedia elements**—Make an honest assessment as to whether the multimedia elements you are planning actually benefit the visitor. I have been to many websites with needless multimedia.

- **Don't assume everyone has a super-computer and a high-speed connection**—Just because you have a fast computer, don't assume everyone else does. Keep your multimedia elements simple so that people with slower computers and slower download speeds can still enjoy your site.

- **Choose standard formats**—If possible, keep to the formats mentioned in Chapter 12. These file formats work on the largest number of computers and cause the fewest problems for your visitors. If you can, provide more than one format for your multimedia files, and let visitors choose what works best for them.

- **Never depend on multimedia to communicate your message**—Always back up important information in multimedia with text. That way if the multimedia doesn't work correctly, the visitor still has access to the important information contained in the multimedia file.

- **Clearly label adult content**—If your multimedia files contain images or audio that might not be for everyone, it is a good idea to label that content. No one wants something inappropriate coming out of his speakers at work.

- **Test, test, test**—As mentioned in Chapter 16, "Testing Your Website," testing is important for your website. Testing a multimedia website is even more important.

Using Multimedia

As discussed in Chapter 12, you can provide multimedia in either of two types: downloadable and streaming.

With downloadable files, you save the multimedia file to your web server and then place a link on one of your web pages. When someone visits your site and clicks on the link, the file is downloaded to the visitor's computer. The visitor then uses a media player to play that web file. The drawback of using

21

downloadable files is that the visitor has to leave your website to experience your multimedia file. Also, after the file is downloaded, you lose control over it. Users who download your multimedia files now have their own copies of it. If you are making your living from these multimedia files, you might not want to share them with everyone.

With streaming files, visitors to your website click on a multimedia link, and a media player runs within their browser (usually a browser plug-in) to play the multimedia file. Streaming files are more difficult to set up than downloadable files, but they have the advantage of keeping visitors at your site and preventing them from downloading your multimedia files. You can also use the method of using another server with many video websites, such as YouTube.com (see Figure 21.2).

FIGURE 21.2
There are millions of videos on YouTube.com.

Storing Multimedia Files

You can store your multimedia files in one of two places: on your server or on someone else's. The location you choose depends on your needs and resources.

If you store your multimedia files on your server, you first must make sure you have the space and bandwidth available to store these files. Multimedia files can be quite large, and large files require a great deal of bandwidth.

You also can store multimedia files on someone else's server. For example, when you put a video file on YouTube, you are storing that file on YouTube's web server. There are certain advantages and disadvantages to doing this. If you use YouTube to post a video file, the site's wealth of server space and bandwidth makes that file easily available, but it also might have a policy that limits file sizes. Regardless of where you post your files, you'll always be at the mercy of the server, which can go down for a while and make your files inaccessible.

Now that you understand how to use and store multimedia files, let's explore how to download and stream them. It's best to be familiar with using both downloadable and streaming files, so the following sections explain each method in detail. The first section explains how to link to multimedia files, and the second section explains how to use an embedded player in a browser to play your multimedia files.

Downloading Audio and Video Files

To allow people to download a file, you need to create a link to that file and allow visitors to save it to their computers or play it immediately in the player associated with that file type. The first thing to do is create an audio file and put it on your web server. Then create a web page that links to that file. When someone visits your page and then clicks on the link, the browser asks visitors whether to save the file or play it. If they choose Download, the file is saved on the visitor's hard drive, and any compatible player can be used to play it. If the visitor chooses to play the file, the browser starts the associated application, and the visitor hears the audio after it is downloaded.

To create a link to an audio file, follow these steps:

1. Create your audio file and save it to your hard drive.

2. Move that audio file to your web server.

3. Create a page with the following code:

```
<html>
<title>Link To Audio File</title>
<body>
    Use this <A href="audio.wav">link</A> to download an audio
➥file.
</body>
</html>
```

4. Save the HTML code as audio.html in the same folder as the audio file (see Figure 21.3).

5. Test!

21

FIGURE 21.3

A simple audio download link page.

As you can see, downloading audio and video is simple.

Streaming Audio and Video

Streaming audio and video requires a bit more work. When creating a streaming audio or video link, you need to embed the player as well as link to the file.

Streaming audio and video requires some programming and requires the creation of complex links to other sites that can play your audio or video files remotely. Here are some resources to help you:

- **XSPF Web Music Player**—http://musicplayer.sourceforge.net
- **iLike**—www.ilike.com/garageband
- **Streamalot**—www.streamalot.com/wm-embed.shtml
- **Embedded MP3 Audio Player**—www.macloo.com/examples/audio_player

Instead of doing all the work yourself, there are now video-hosting sites that allow you to play and reference your videos. The best part is that the video-hosting sites (like YouTube.com) have made streaming easy for you. Here are the steps:

1. Create your video file and save it to your hard drive.
2. Go to YouTube.com and create an account: www.youtube.com/signup?next=. Creating an account enables you to upload videos (see Figure 21.4).
3. After you have a YouTube.com account, log in and click the Upload button. This opens the video upload screen.
4. Enter the appropriate information for your video, and upload the file. YouTube lets you upload a number of video types, but take note that the file needs to be less than a gigabyte and less than 10 minutes in length (unless you have a special YouTube account).
5. After your video is uploaded, you will notice that on the page for the video is an area called Embed, as shown in Figure 21.5. This area contains the code you need to add this YouTube video on any web page.

21

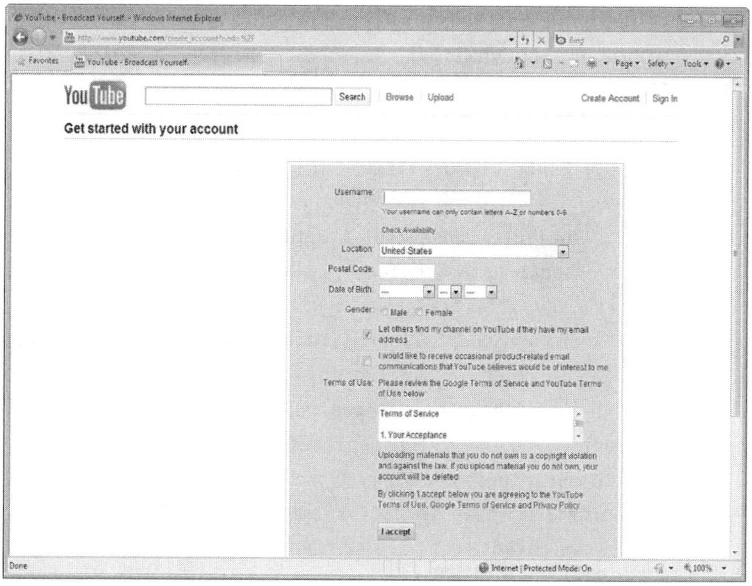

FIGURE 21.4
The YouTube account signup page.

FIGURE 21.5
Notice the Embed link on the bottom of the video.

6. Create a blank web page, and add the embed text in the body of your page. For example:

```
<html>

<title>Party Video</title>
<body>
        <object width="640" height="385">
        <param name="movie" value="http://www.youtube.com/v/
➡-xL7YSsEyOs?fs=1&amp;hl=en_US"></param>
        <param name="allowFullScreen" value="true"></param>
        <param name="allowscriptaccess" value="always"></param>
        <embed src="http://www.youtube.com/v/-xL7YSsEyOs?fs=
➡1&amp;hl=en_US" type="application/x-shockwave-flash"
➡allowscriptaccess="always" allowfullscreen="true"
➡width="640" height="385"></embed>
        </object>
</body>
</html>
```

7. Save your web page, view it, and you will see the video (see Figure 21.6).

FIGURE 21.6

A page with an embedded YouTube video.

Advanced Multimedia Options

Audio and video make your website come alive, and now you can create interactive multimedia elements for your website without spending money or learning a programming language.

This area is a bit of a gold rush right now. Many companies are trying to make as much money as possible making easy-to-use multimedia apps and widgets. There are still some great options available for free, but they require some looking around.

In the previous edition of this book, I featured Sprout Builder, which is now a pay service with different features. Now I'll introduce you to a few websites offering multimedia features that you can use with your website.

> **caution**   This area is changing constantly, and sites come in and out of existence without much warning. Also, as with Sprout Builder, sites can suddenly start to charge for their services.

Wix.com (www.wix.com)

Wix.com allows you to create a free multimedia, flash-based website. The Wix editor makes creating simple, clean sites with multimedia widgets easy. Their templates are professional, and the interface is easy to use.

Webtrends Apps (www.transpond.com/)

Webtrends offers a range of the latest apps. These include multimedia, social, and conversation apps. Each app has an example and then steps you through the process of building it. This option is a bit more technical but still is not as complex as programming.

Advanced Open-Source Multimedia

If you need something more complicated than Sprout allows, there is an open-source alternative to the expensive programs such as Macromedia Flash. OpenLaszlo (www.openlaszlo.org, see Figure 21.7) is an open-source program that allows you to develop advanced, robust multimedia websites. This program is not for the beginner, but it can help you build amazing multimedia websites. It requires scripting, programming, and graphics skills.

21

FIGURE 21.7

The OpenLaszlo home page.

Building a Site Using a Wiki

A wiki is an editable set of web pages that enable users to collaborate to create a site that organizes information. The word *wiki* is a Hawaiian word for fast. The idea is that anyone can change a wiki page quickly. Ward Cunningham created the first wiki in 1994, but the wiki really began to take off when Wikipedia was created in 2001.

The subject matter for a wiki can be anything—and I do mean anything. There are wikis about camping trips, television shows, online games, and car racing, to name a few. Any time people need to collaborate on creating an information source, a wiki is an excellent choice.

This chapter covers how to use a website called PBworks and open-source software called MediaWiki to build your own wiki. PBworks is a website that enables you to create wikis, and MediaWiki software installs on your own web host and enables you to run and manage your own wiki.

note Wikipedia (see Figure 22.1) is the most famous wiki in the world. It is the largest open-source knowledge project the world has ever seen. It has more than 2.5 million articles in English, and millions of dedicated users.

There are distinct differences between PBworks and MediaWiki. To help you decide which is best for you, I've created lists of reasons to use each. These lists will help you determine your priorities and decide which section of this chapter you should read.

FIGURE 22.1
Wikipedia is the most famous wiki on the Internet.

Five Reasons to Use PBworks to Host Your Wiki

- **You are new to wikis**—PBworks makes it easy to get up and running quickly while connecting you to a larger community of more experienced wiki creators.

- **You have low technical ability**—PBworks is a nice and easy way to take advantage of some complicated technology that you never have to worry about.

- **You don't want to spend money for a wiki**—A basic PBworks wiki is free for three or fewer users. You can't save more money than that!

22

■ **You don't care about bells and whistles**—If you want a simple, well-run, robust wiki and don't care about the latest gadgets or add-ins, PBworks is for you.

■ **You don't need your own domain**—PBworks' wikis are hosted under the PBworks.com domain. If you're okay with not having your own domain, PBworks is a good choice for you.

Five Reasons to Use MediaWiki for Your Wiki

■ **You have your own domain**—If you want a specific domain name, use MediaWiki, because its software has no domain name restrictions.

■ **You want a lot of people to edit your wiki**—MediaWiki has no restrictions on how many people can edit your wiki.

■ **You care about bells and whistles**—If you want to control every detail of your wiki, you might want to download the MediaWiki software.

■ **You have technical knowledge**—Installing, configuring, and using MediaWiki software requires knowledge of some technical things.

■ **Your hosting service offers MediaWiki installs**—Your hosting services let you automatically install MediaWiki. This gives you control and easy installation.

What Is PBworks?

PBworks (formerly PBwiki) is a website that offers hosting of education and business collaborative spaces. The original name is meant to imply that creating a wiki on the PBwiki site is as easy as creating a peanut butter sandwich, but the company has since branded its product as a collaborative workspace. More than half a million wikis exist on PBworks (see Figure 22.2). The site allows quick wiki creation and use without requiring you to run the wiki software on your own host. You can also browse its lists of blogs and find out who else is using the site.

PBworks offers free wikis (or collaborative workspaces) to personal and educational users. If you need to create a wiki for profit, you must pay for the service or choose another alternative.

FIGURE 22.2
The PBworks home page.

Building a Wiki Using PBworks

If you want to use a basic version of a wiki and want someone else to take care of all your hosting needs, PBworks.com is a good solution. This section of the chapter covers getting a wiki up and running on PBworks.com.

Before you begin at PBworks.com, you need the following:

- An idea for your wiki
- A name for your wiki
- An email address

Signing Up for PBworks

To begin using PBworks.com, you need to sign up for the service. It is 100% free to personal and educational users (but only if you have fewer than three users) and gives you access to its software and a whole community of people using PBworks.com.

1. Open your web browser and navigate to www.PBworks.com. This opens the home page for PBworks, where you sign up for the wiki hosting service.

caution Because PBworks.com is a website that is constantly being updated, these instructions may differ from what you see.

2. Click the For Personal link. The PBworks for Personal Use information page is displayed. Read this carefully, and click the Sign Up Now button. The Sign Up page appears (see Figure 22.3). On this page, you enter all the information you need to set up your wiki on the PBworks servers.

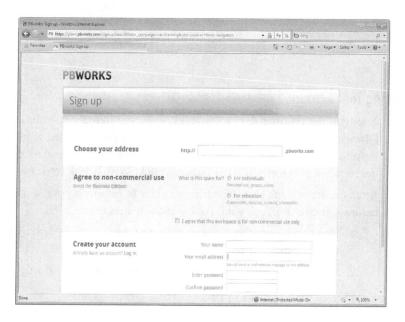

FIGURE 22.3

The Sign Up page.

3. Enter the address you want to use for your workspace in the Choose Your Address field.

4. Agree to use the workspace noncommercially, such as for personal or educational use.

5. In the Your Name field, enter your name.

6. In the Your Email Address field, enter your email address. PBworks uses your email address to communicate information and administrative notes. Make sure it is correct.

7. In the Enter Password field, enter a word or phrase. Make your password unique and easy to remember, and try to have a mixture of letters and numbers. The case of the letters matters also, so use a mixture of upper- and lowercase.

8. In the Confirm Password field, enter your password again. Choose a wiki name, and enter it in the Wiki Name field. This also becomes the URL to your wiki, so it can't have spaces and should be letters and numbers only.

9. Click the Next button.

10. Check your email for a confirmation, and follow the instructions carefully.

Activating Your Account

After you have signed up for PBworks, you need to activate your account. PBworks will have sent an email to the address you provided when you were signing up. When you receive the email message, read it and follow the instructions in the email. This includes clicking on a link to activate your wiki.

After you have done this, PBworks asks you to establish your security settings before you can use your wiki. Follow these instructions:

1. Select who can view your workspace (either anyone or only people you invite or approve).

2. Select who can edit your workspace (either anyone or only people you invite or approve).

3. Take the time to read a stunningly exciting set of Terms of Service.

4. Click the box saying you agree to the PBworks Terms of Service.

5. Click the Take Me to My Workspace button. Your new workspace is displayed (see Figure 22.4). To begin, the front page of your workspace is displayed. This page, like any page on your wiki, is editable by you. Because you are a registered user and the owner of this wiki, you have options along the right side—things such as adding a new page and uploading files.

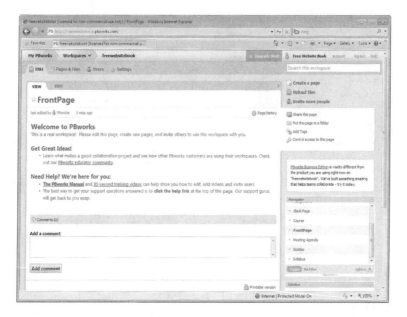

FIGURE 22.4

Your new PBworks workspace.

Editing a Page

The power of wikis is apparent in the ability you have to edit the pages to share information with all visitors. Editing PBworks pages is easy. After you turn on Edit mode for your wiki page, you have a WYSIWYG (what you see is what you get) editor for that page. Follow these instructions to turn on Edit mode:

1. Click the tab at the top of the page that says Edit to open the page in Edit mode (see Figure 22.5). Edit mode enables you to edit your PBworks page.

2. Now you can edit all the text on the page. Across the top of the edit area is a formatting toolbar that enables you to format your text.

3. When you're finished, click the Save button. The edits you made have now taken effect.

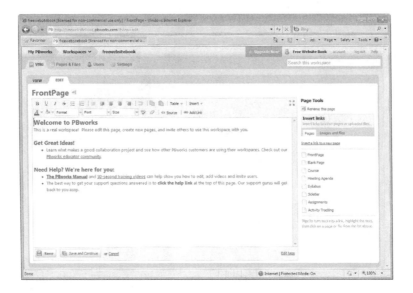

FIGURE 22.5

Edit mode for a wiki page.

Adding a Page

PBworks also enables you to add pages easily. These pages help you organize information and enable you to expand your PBworks. Follow these instructions to add a page:

1. Click the Create Page button on the top-right corner of the page. This opens the page where you name your new wiki page (see Figure 22.6).

2. Enter the name of the page, and click Create Page. You are then presented with a blank page with your title on it. Edit and save the new page as instructed in the preceding section.

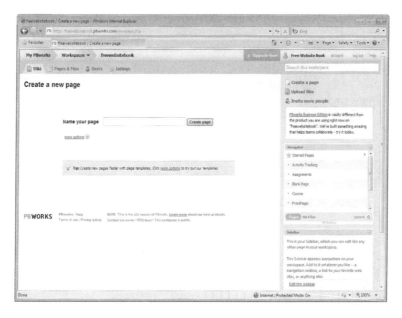

FIGURE 22.6

Use this page to add the name of your new page.

Linking Pages

After you have more than one page, you'll want to create links to multiple pages. You do this in the Edit mode. Follow these steps to add a link:

1. Open a page in Edit mode.
2. Enter some text for the hyperlink.
3. Click the Link button in the Formatting toolbar. This opens the Create Link window (see Figure 22.7).
4. Click on the Browse Pages & Files link and from the Link Type list, select PBworks page.
5. In the Page Name box, select the page to which you want to link. If it is a new page, you can enter the name in the Name field.
6. Click OK. Your new link is created.

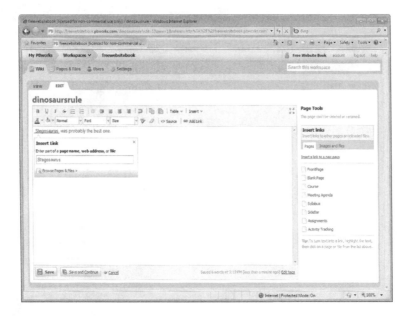

FIGURE 22.7

Use this window to add a link.

Viewing Page History

One of the most powerful features of a wiki is page history. This means that a copy of every version of a wiki page is kept and can be compared to every other version of that page. For example, if you make a change to a wiki page and then come back in a few hours and see it has changed again, a wiki page history can tell you the exact changes that were made, who made them, and when. You also can then revert to any one of those previous versions of the page. If you have a moment, look at the history of a Wikipedia page, and you will see how much work actually goes into creating it. To view a page's history, click the View History button at the top of the page. This then shows you the page's history (see Figure 22.8).

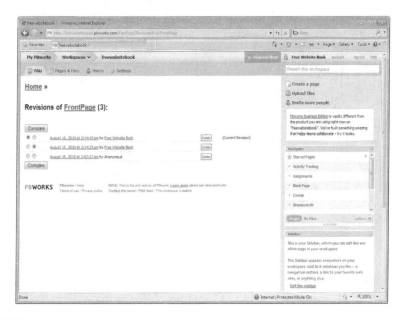

FIGURE 22.8

This is the history for a PBworks page.

Setting Up Your Own Wiki Using MediaWiki Software

If you've already tried the PBworks solution but want to expand the functions, the look, or the feel of your wiki, or maybe you're more of a techie geek and you want something more than PBworks has to offer, MediaWiki is for you.

MediaWiki enables you to install and configure your wiki (see Figure 22.9). There are a number of different open-source wiki software programs—MediaWiki, TikiWiki, and FlexWiki, to name a few. I am going to cover MediaWiki because it is the same software used to run Wikipedia and it's an excellent example of a wiki.

caution When installing software on your own, there is a possibility that things will go wrong or might not work as expected. It's crucial to back up anything important before beginning this process, just in case.

FIGURE 22.9
The MediaWiki home page.

Information You Need Before You Begin

After you have decided to install your own MediaWiki software, you need to do a few things before you begin.

MediaWiki Software Architecture

Like the WordPress software discussed in Chapter 19, "Building a Blog Using WordPress," the MediaWiki software uses scripts written in PHP and MySQL for a database. For a high-level view of this architecture, with an explanation of the parts, see Chapter 19.

Before Installing Your MediaWiki Software

Before starting your install of MediaWiki software, you need some tools, and you need to do some simple things with your hosting service.

note Without access to PHP and MySQL on your web server, you cannot run MediaWiki software. If one of these pieces is missing, you need to use PBworks or look for another wiki solution.

If you need help finding a host, refer to Chapter 2, "Choosing a Location for Your Site." Here's what you need to do before installing the MediaWiki software:

1. Check to see that the right software is installed on your server. To run MediaWiki 1.13.2, your web hosting service has to provide the following:

   ■ PHP version 5.0 or greater (5.1.x is recommended)

   ■ MySQL version 4.0 or greater

2. Get a text editor. You might have to edit some text files to get your MediaWiki install up and running. A text file is simply a file with words and numbers in it that doesn't contain formatting. For more information about good text editors, refer to Chapter 5, "Gathering Your Tools."

3. Get an FTP client. FTP stands for File Transfer Protocol and is a fancy name for the software that allows you to easily transfer files between machines. When you are installing software such as MediaWiki, you need to be able to move files between machines easily. An FTP client is a program that helps you do this. For more information about good FTP clients, refer to Chapter 5.

4. Pick a username and password that are unique and contain letters and numbers.

Download and Install MediaWiki

Similar to more complex software we have covered (Joomla and WordPress), you need to download the MediWiki software to your computer and install it on your web server. Follow these steps:

1. Download the MediaWiki software. Go to www.mediawiki.org/wiki/Download (see Figure 22.10).

2. Click to download MediaWiki 1.16.0 or the latest version.

3. Navigate to the correct version directory (1.13.2).

4. A *tar.gz* file is downloaded to your computer.

5. Unzip this file to your hard drive.

Geek Speak

tar.gz file

A tar.gz file is a special type of zip file. You need a program that opens zip files, such as WinZip or 7zip. For more information, consult Chapter 5.

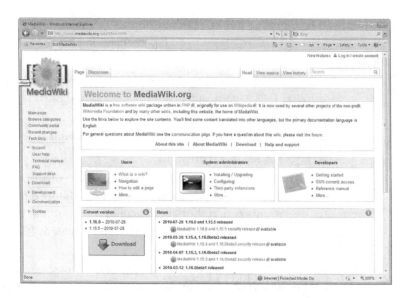

FIGURE 22.10
The MediaWiki download page.

From this point on, you can refer to the MediaWiki installation documentation to install and configure MediaWiki. Here are some additional documentation sources to help you with your installation:

- **MediaWiki Manual:Installation Guide**—www.mediawiki.org/wiki/Manual:Installation

- **Installing Mediawiki Is Much Easier Than the Instructions Suggest**—My Quick 10 Step Tutorial for Installing Mediawiki—www.idratherbewriting.com/2007/06/14/installing-mediawiki-is-much-easier-than-the-instructions-suggest-my-quick-10-step-tutorial-for-installing-mediawiki

- **Creating and Publishing Web Pages**— www.washington.edu/computing/web/publishing/mediawiki.html

After you have downloaded and installed MediaWiki, its operation is similar to that of PBwiki, with quite a few added features and no limitation on size or number of users. Here are a few additional MediaWiki resources:

- **MediaWiki Help:Contents**—www.mediawiki.org/wiki/Help:Contents

- **Using MediaWiki**—www.deakin.edu.au/itl/dso/guides/qg-mediawiki-userguide.html

- **MediaWiki User Guide**—http://en.wikibooks.org/wiki/MediaWiki_User_Guide

Keep an Eye on Things

MediaWiki is a dynamic wiki software program that is always changing and improving. Keep a close eye on your MediaWiki software announcements. Take part in the MediaWiki community, wiki your hearts out, and most importantly have lots of fun!

Appendixes

List of the Most Common HTML Tags

This is a list of some of the most commonly used HTML tags. Remember, you should open and close your tags as shown in Chapter 10, "HTML 101." The tags are listed alphabetically here so you can find what you are looking for.

For this edition, I have added some HTML5 tags. As mentioned earlier, HTML5 is still in development, so it's subject to change, but I wanted to give you a heads up on some of the new tags. Also, HTML5 does not work the same in all browsers, so take extra care if using HTML5 to check in as many browsers as possible.

Table A.1 Common HTML Tags

Tag	Usage
` `	Code for a nonbreaking space
`<!-- -->`	Comments
`<a href="index.html">`	Creating links
`<b></b>`	Bold text (will not be supported by HTML5)
`<basefont size= 1> </basefont>`	Set base font size from 1 to 7
`<blockquote></blockquote>`	Separates text
`<body></body>`	Body of HTML
` </br>`	Line break
`<button ...></button>`	Adds a button
`<caption></caption>`	Adds a table caption
`<center></center>`	Centers text (will not be supported by HTML5)
`<div></div>`	Division of code
`<em></em>`	Adds emphasis or bolding
`<font></font>`	Selects font
`<frameset></frameset>`	Start of fames
`<h1></h1>`	Heading 1, which is the largest heading size; normally used for titles
`<h2></h2>`	Heading 2
`<h3></h3>`	Heading 3
`<h4></h4>`	Heading 4
`<h5></h5>`	Heading 5
`<h6></h6>`	Heading 6
`<head></head>`	Head of HTML document
`<hr></hr>`	Horizontal line
`<html></html>`	Start of any HTML document
`<i></i>`	Italics
`<iframe></iframe>`	An inline frame
`<img src ="image location></img>`	Image source
`<input name></input>`	Input form
`<li></li>`	List item

Tag	Usage
`<meta name= ></meta>`	Meta information
`<ol></ol>`	Numbered list
`<option value="list"></option>`	Option form
`<p></p>`	New paragraph
`<param></param>`	Sets a parameter on an element
`<q></q>`	Quotation
`<select name></select>`	Selection form
`<strike></strike>`	Strikethrough text (will not be supported by HTML5)
`<style></style>`	Style sheet definition
`<sub></sub>`	Subscript text
`<sup></sup>`	Superscript text
`<table></table>`	Table definition
`<td></td>`	Data cell definition
`<th></th>`	Header cell for a table
`<title></title>`	Document title
`<tr></tr>`	Table row
`<ul></ul>`	Bulleted list

Table A.2   HTML5 Tags

Tag	Usage
`<article></article>`	Semantic tag for article body
`<footer></footer>`	Semantic tag for page footer
`<header></header>`	Semantic tag for page header
`<nav></nav>`	Semantic tag for navigation elements
`<section></section>`	Semantic tag for sections

Free and Open-Source Software Sites

created this appendix to give you one place to go to for open-source websites. These links include sites covering the history of open source, news, and open-source tools. This is by no means a comprehensive list—new sites pop up every day—but hopefully these sites will act as an excellent starting point.

note The Internet is a dynamic place, and some of these links might have changed. If the links are incorrect, search for the title in Google and drop me a line with the new link.

History of Open Source

- **Open Source Wikipedia entry**—http://en.wikipedia.org/wiki/Open_source
- **History of Free Software Wikipedia page**—http://en.wikipedia.org/wiki/History_of_free_software
- **Brief History of Open Source**—http://www.netc.org/openoptions/background/history.html

Open-Source News

- **Linux.com**—http://www.linux.com/
- **Yahoo! Linux/Open Source News**—http://news.yahoo.com/technology/linux-open-source
- **TecTonic**—http://www.tectonic.co.za/

General Open-Source Sites

- **Open Source Windows**—http://www.opensourcewindows.org/
- **Open Source Mac**—http://www.opensourcemac.org/
- **Open Source as Alternative**—http://www.osalt.com/
- **The Top 50 Proprietary Programs That Drive You Crazy—and Their Open Source Alternatives**—http://whdb.com/2008/the-top-50-proprietary-programs-that-drive-you-crazy-and-their-open-source-alternatives/

Operating Systems

- **Linux**—http://www.linux.org/
- **Ubuntu**—http://www.ubuntu.com/
- **Qimo**—http://www.qimo4kids.com/

Web Browsers

- **Firefox**—http://www.firefox.com/
- **Google Chrome**—http://www.google.com/chrome

Office Suites

- OpenOffice—http://www.openoffice.org/
- NeoOffice—http://www.neooffice.org/

File Transfer Tools

- FileZilla (Windows, Linux, and Mac)—http://filezilla-project.org/
- Fetch (Mac)—http://fetchsoftworks.com/
- Cyberduck (Mac)—http://cyberduck.ch/
- OneButton FTP (Mac)—http://onebutton.org/
- Net2ftp—http://www.net2ftp.com/

Text Editors

- Notepad ++ (Windows, Linux)—http://notepad-plus.sourceforge.net/uk/site.htm
- TextWrangler (Mac)—http://www.barebones.com/products/textwrangler/index.shtml
- XEmacs (Windows. Linux, UNIX)—http://www.xemacs.org/index.html

Graphics Editors

- Gimp (Windows, Mac, Linux)—http://www.gimp.org/
- Inkscape (Windows, Mac, Linux)—http://inkscape.org/
- Paint.Net (Windows)—http://www.getpaint.net/
- Seashore (Mac OS X)—http://seashore.sourceforge.net/

HTML Editors

- KompoZer (Windows, Mac, Linux)—http://www.kompozer.net/
- Quanta Plus (Windows, Linux)—http://quanta.kdewebdev.org/
- Bluefish (Windows, Mac, Linux)—http://bluefish.openoffice.nl/
- SeaMonkey (Windows, Mac, Linux)—http://www.seamonkey-project.org/

- OpenLaszlo (Windows, Mac, Linux)—http://www.openlaszlo.org/
- CSSED (Windows, Linux)—http://cssed.sourceforge.net/
- NVU (Windows, Mac, Linux)—http://nvudev.com/index.php

Video Editors

- Avidemux—http://fixounet.free.fr/avidemux/
- Blender—http://www.blender.org/
- Cinefx—http://www.cinefx.org/
- Cinelerra—http://cinelerra.org

Sound Recording

- Audacity (Windows, Mac, Linux)—http://audacity.sourceforge.net/

Web Servers

- The Apache Software Foundation—http://www.apache.org/
- Savant Web Server—http://savant.sourceforge.net/
- Roxen WebServer—http://www.roxen.com/products/cms/webserver/

Database Tools

- phpMyAdmin (Web Utility)—http://www.phpmyadmin.net/
- MySQL—http://www.mysql.com/

Blog Software

- WordPress.com—http://wordpress.com/
- LifeType—http://lifetype.net/
- Movable Type—http://www.movabletype.com/

CMS Software

- **Drupal**—http://drupal.org/
- **Joomla!**—http://www.joomla.org/
- **OpensourceCMS**—http://opensourcecms.com/
- **Liferay**—http://www.liferay.com

Wiki Software

- **Media Wiki**—http://MediaWiki.org
- **TWiki**—http://twiki.org/
- **PBWorks**—http://pbwiki.com/
- **Wetpaint**—http://www.wetpaint.com/

Script Tools

- **EasyPHP (Web Utility)**—http://www.easyphp.org/

Index

B

M

U

V

W

FREE Online Edition

Your purchase of **Build a Website for Free** includes access to a free online edition for 45 days through the Safari Books Online subscription service. Nearly every Que book is available online through Safari Books Online, along with more than 5,000 other technical books and videos from publishers such as Addison-Wesley Professional, Cisco Press, Exam Cram, IBM Press, O'Reilly, Prentice Hall, and Sams.

SAFARI BOOKS ONLINE allows you to search for a specific answer, cut and paste code, download chapters, and stay current with emerging technologies.

Activate your FREE Online Edition at
www.informit.com/safarifree

> **STEP 1:** Enter the coupon code: WEKGNCB.

> **STEP 2:** New Safari users, complete the brief registration form.
> Safari subscribers, just log in.

If you have difficulty registering on Safari or accessing the online edition,
please e-mail customer-service@safaribooksonline.com